MW00655234

LIQUID CONSPIRACY

JFK, LSD, THE CIA, AREA 51, AND UFOS

The **Mind Control/Conspiracy Series:**
- MIND CONTROL, WORLD CONTROL
- INSIDE THE GEMSTONE FILE
- NASA, NAZIS, & JFK
- LIQUID CONSPIRACY
- MIND CONTROL, OSWALD & JFK
- HAARP: THE ULTIMATE WEAPON OF THE CONSPIRACY

The **New Science Series:**
- THE TIME TRAVEL HANDBOOK
- THE FREE ENERGY DEVICE HANDBOOK
- THE FANTASTIC INVENTIONS OF NIKOLA TESLA
- THE ANTI-GRAVITY HANDBOOK
- ANTI-GRAVITY & THE WORLD GRID
- ANTI-GRAVITY & THE UNIFIED FIELD
- ETHER TECHNOLOGY
- THE ENERGY GRID
- THE BRIDGE TO INFINITY
- THE HARMONIC CONQUEST OF SPACE
- VIMANA AIRCRAFT OF ANCIENT INDIA & ATLANTIS
- UFOS & ANTI-GRAVITY: Piece For a Jig-Saw
- THE COSMIC MATRIX: Piece For a Jig-Saw, Part II

The **Mystic Traveller Series:**
- IN SECRET TIBET by Theodore Illion (1937)
- DARKNESS OVER TIBET by Theodore Illion (1938)
- IN SECRET MONGOLIA by Henning Haslund (1934)
- MEN AND GODS IN MONGOLIA by Henning Haslund (1935)
- MYSTERY CITIES OF THE MAYA by Thomas Gann (1925)
- THE MYSTERY OF EASTER ISLAND by Katherine Routledge (1919)
- SECRET CITIES OF OLD SOUTH AMERICA by Harold Wilkins (1952)

The **Lost Cities Series:**
- LOST CITIES OF ATLANTIS, ANCIENT EUROPE
  & THE MEDITERRANEAN
- LOST CITIES OF NORTH & CENTRAL AMERICA
- LOST CITIES & ANCIENT MYSTERIES OF SOUTH AMERICA
- LOST CITIES OF ANCIENT LEMURIA & THE PACIFIC
- LOST CITIES & ANCIENT MYSTERIES OF AFRICA & ARABIA
- LOST CITIES OF CHINA, CENTRAL ASIA & INDIA

LIQUID CONSPIRACY

BY
GEORGE PICCARD

FOREWORD BY
KENN THOMAS

Liquid Conspiracy

Copyright 1999

George Piccard

Foreword Copyright 1999
by Kenn Thomas

First Printing

June 1999

ISBN 0-932813-57-7

Printed in Canada

Published by
Adventures Unlimited Press
One Adventure Place
Kempton, Illinois 60946   USA
auphq@frontiernet.net

10 9 8 7 6 5 4 3 2

LIQUID CONSPIRACY

JFK, LSD, THE CIA, AREA 51, AND UFOS

CONTENTS

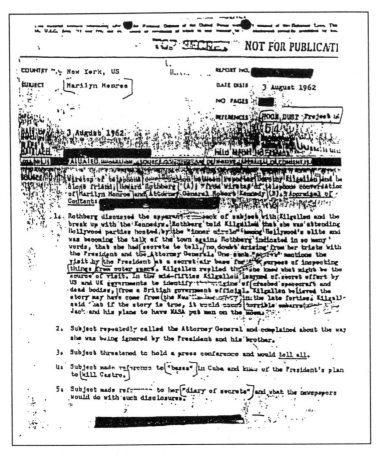

TOP SECRET   NOT FOR PUBLICATI

COUNTRY: New York, US

SUBJECT: Marilyn Monroe

REPORT NO.: ▓▓▓▓

DATE DISTR: 3 August 1962

NO PAGES: ▓▓

REFERENCES: ROGN DUST Project 1▓

DATE: 3 August 1962

SOURCE: ▓▓

Wiretap of telephone conversation between reporter Dorothy Kilgallen and a close friend, Howard Rothberg (A) from Wiretap of telephone conversation of Marilyn Monroe and Attorney General Robert Kennedy (B). Appraisal of Contents:

1. Rothberg discussed the apparent break of subject with Kilgallen and the break up with the Kennedys. Rothberg told Kilgallen that she was attending Hollywood parties hosted by the "inner circle" among Hollywood's elite and was becoming the talk of the town again. Rothberg indicated in so many words, that she had secrets to tell, no doubt arising from her trists with the President and the Attorney General. One such "secret" mentions the visit by the President at a secret air base for the purpose of inspecting things from outer space. Kilgallen replied the she knew what might be the source of visit. In the mid-fifties Kilgallen learned of secret effort by US and UK governments to identify the origins of crashed spacecraft and dead bodies, from a British government official. Kilgallen believed the story may have come from the New ▓▓▓▓▓▓▓ in the late forties. Kilgallen said that if the story is true, it would cause terrible embarrassment for Jack and his plans to have NASA put men on the moon.

2. Subject repeatedly called the Attorney General and complained about the way she was being ignored by the President and his brother.

3. Subject threatened to hold a press conference and would tell all.

4. Subject made reference to "bases" in Cuba and knew of the President's plan to kill Castro.

5. Subject made reference to her "diary of secrets" and what the newspapers would do with such disclosures.

▓▓▓▓▓▓▓▓▓▓▓▓▓▓▓▓▓▓▓▓▓▓▓▓▓▓▓

A "Top Secret" report on Marilyn Monroe and Dorothy Killgallen. It is a memoranda discussing a transcript of a wiretapped conversation between Howard Rothberg and Dorothy Kilgallen, the newspaper columnist quoted by Lincoln Lawrence who referred to Reich's cloudbusting as a means of mind control. Kilgallen and Rothberg discuss Marilyn Monroe's claim that JFK took her to "a secret airbase for the purpose of inspecting things from outer space." Reich had used cloudbusting in his encounters with UFOs. Killgallen was later murdered.

FOREWORD

by Kenn Thomas

The first image conjured by George Piccard's concept of "Liquid Conspiracy," of course, is that of blotter acid. While Piccard covers much more ground than the history of LSD, his title does remind readers that powerful psychoactive substances play an important role in the history of conspiracies. Abuse of psychedelics and other drugs became the central activity of the notorious brainwashing programs ARTICHOKE and MKULTRA, for instance. Psychedelic stalwarts like Tim Leary gave the CIA great credit for ushering in the psychedelic era by providing the first acid to Beat luminaries such as himself, Ken Kesey, Allen Ginsberg and the like. Unfortunately, the CIA also ushered in that era for others—unsuspecting test subjects like Dr. Frank Olsen, whose case Piccard discusses—who did not welcome it, who did not know, in fact, that the drugs had been slipped to them. Piccard does a good review of that history and provides some new details about the infamous and ongoing intelligence community interest in mind-altering substances.

Piccard only goes there briefly, however. The Liquid Conspiracy he relates here actually starts with a secret meeting in Switzerland in 1945, allying different power elites whose competitions extend back to the beginning of civilization and expect to exert influence far into the future. This is the bad acid trip of the modern era, the military-industrial-corporate nightmare that rains bombs almost at random in "problem areas" like Yugoslavia and Iraq, just to keep an impossible war economy rolling.

The Liquid Conspiracy is Area 51, Cheyenne Mountain, Pine Gap, the interlocking tunnel systems that connect vast bunkers and underground facilities around the country. It's black helicopters and mind control implants. It's television brainwash and high school violence, where towns whose citizens primarily are employed by Lockheed's intercontinental ballistic missile system wonder why

9

terrible violence breaks out at one of its high schools. It's Jim Jones and Charles Manson all right, but it's also Heaven's Gate, Art Bell, the remote viewers, the thinly veiled military propaganda message of such popular movies as *Independence Day* and *Conspiracy Theory*, TV shows like *X Files* and *Star Trek*, and Bill Clinton's $100 billion Star Wars restart. As Piccard says, "the Liquid Conspiracy has employed millions of persons, directly and indirectly, in its various attempts to create total world control."

The surrealism of civilization's current predicament swims in the liquid conspiracy. Take, for instance, the circumstances that surround Lee Harvey Oswald's known involvement with LSD. Oswald did some of his military service at the Atsugi Naval Base in Japan, and a fellow member of his unit acknowledged involvement in human-subject LSD military experiments. (Interestingly, the U2 reconnaissance plane flew out of Atsugi; Oswald provided information on the U2 that facilitated the Soviet shoot down of Gary Powers; and the U2 was developed at Area 51.)

In 1962, Oswald entered the offices of an assistant attorney in New Orleans named Ed Gillen and confessed that he knew an LSD supplier and wanted to find out about the legal status of the drug. Oswald also talked about Aldous Huxley, the great author of such psychedelic literature classics as *Brave New World* and *Heaven or Hell*, books later discovered to have been checked out of the library by Oswald. Students of the JFK assassination look with suspicion on Oswald's surprisingly public announcement of his interest in drugs—but it was really only the first ripple in the liquid

Just as Oswald may have been faking an interest in LSD, he may have also faked an interest in anti-Castro activity through the Fair Play for Cuba Committee, and that's when the story really takes on psychedelic dimensions. Another person, named John Robert Glenn, also developed an ersatz connection with that committee, illegally traveling to Cuba with 58 other students in 1963. (Bob Dylan thanked this group when he accepted the Tom Paine Award from the Emergency Civil Liberties Committee that year. In the same speech, he was booed for expressing sympathy for Oswald.)

Glenn became one of many "second Oswalds" that proliferate in the lore about the president's alleged assassin, having been picked up by police in Indianapolis who had connected him to a rifle that may have been used in the shooting. Another second Oswald, Robert Webster of Zelionople, Pennsylvania, even defected and spent time in the Soviet Union, as Oswald had and during the same period. Oswald's time in Minsk, in fact, may have involved a non-drug mind control technology called RHIC (Radio Hypnotic Intracerebral Control) and EDOM (Electronic Dissolution of Memory), a story first told in Lincoln Lawrence's 1968 book *Were We Controlled?*, reprinted by Adventures Unlimited Press, with new annotations, as *Mind Control, Oswald and JFK*.

Multiple Oswalds appear on the scene in Dallas on November 22, at a car dealership, on the gun range and elsewhere, like a cloning experiment that got out of hand. The great Discordian Kerry Thornley was one of many second Oswalds identified by New Orleans DA Jim Garrison. With his connections to the spy world and the extremely unlikely turn of events that brought his early death and gave him immortality, Oswald could not have had a more hallucinatory life experience if he had dropped LSD for breakfast daily.

Acid occupies a central place in the story of Mary Pinchot Meyer as well, touched upon by Piccard in his chapter on "Sex, Drugs and UFOs." Meyer apparently took LSD with JFK in her role as his last lover. She also supposedly belonged to a clique of Washington women whose ambition was to stop the military industrial state by having its leaders chill out on psychedelic chemicals. Larger plans loomed for the use of those chemicals, however, and Meyer wound up murdered shortly after JFK, along the tow path near the Potomac River in D.C. Tim Leary tells this part of the story in his 1983 autobiography, *Flashbacks*, but the first biography of Meyer, *A Very Private Woman, The Life and Unsolved Murder of Presidential Mistress Mary Meyer* by Nina Burleigh (Bantam), did not get published until 1998.

Burleigh reaches conventional conclusions about Meyer's murder, and reports that "there is no one who has come forward to say that Mary was involved in any organized effort to 'turn on' powerful men. [*Note*: This makes Dr. Leary *persona non grata*, a "no one," with Burleigh.] That notion had been around since Aldous Huxley started experimenting with the drug, and there was at least one organization in California nominally devoted to the goal. Mary might have spontaneously arrived at the idea herself, however. She was already a bit contemptuous of Washington, and once she had had the LSD experience, she might have decided that it could change the world. While other avid LSD users could only daydream about getting it into the water supply of a large city, Mary was connected enough—by 1960, she was an intimate of the president-elect of the United States—to promote or disseminate the drug at high levels.

Burleigh also notes that: "as Cord Meyer's wife, Mary could have learned about CIA infiltration of various academic and other organizations. No public documents link Cord Meyer to the CIA's extensive drug experiments, but at his level in the hierarchy he would have had access to such information." Cord Meyer had been an activist for the liberal World Federalists in the late 1940s before joining the CIA and beginning work for a globalism of a different sort. He served as CIA station chief in London from 1975 to 1976, where one scurrilous internet rumor has him recruiting a young Bill Clinton. Meyer certainly became involved in setting up European travel/activist programs for young CIA recruits who apparently included feminist Gloria Steinem, as part of the psychological warfare program known as Operation Mockingbird (see Alex Constantine's *Psychic Dictatorship in the USA*, Feral House, 1997).

Cord Meyer also bragged about doing CIA disinfo service to discredit Alfred McCoy's book *The Politics of Heroin in Southeast Asia* (Harper and Row, 1972). This connects that 60s-era psychedelic drug intrigue to the harsh realities of hard drug-running and black profits that characterize much of the covert world today. Liquid Conspiracy all over the place.

Burleigh also reports that Mary Pinchot Meyer underwent Reichian therapy with Dr. Charles Oller of Philadelphia. Research suggests that Wilhelm Reich's orgone therapy had captured the attention of the military, and may have been misapplied to the study of mind control and the liquid conspiracy. Declassified memos from MKULTRA's Sub Project 119 suggest that data from Reich's work on the bio-electric nature of sexuality had been collected for the program, and newspaper columnist Dorothy Kilgallen wrote a column in 1964 asking LBJ to "please check with the state department ... the leaders of our Armed Forces or our chief scientists, to discover what, if anything, we are doing to explore the ramifications of 'cloud-busting' [a technology to manipulate the orgone atmospheric continuum] which in its refined stages means *thought control* ..."

Piccard discusses Kilgallen, and the infamous Spiriglio document in which her friend Marilyn Monroe speaks of JFK taking her to see the "things from outer space" at an Area 51-type base in the desert. Kilgallen's interest in UFOs dated back to a 1947 sighting in Spitzbergen, Norway, and she died under mysterious, JFK-related circumstances in November 1965, a death that was accompanied by an electrical blackout of the eastern seaboard and many attendant UFO sightings. One observation needs to be added to Piccard's analysis of Marilyn Monroe's relationship to the liquid conspiracy intrigue, however: the night after the first reports of Monroe's death began to hit the papers, two women competed for JFK's attention—Judith Campbell and Mary Pinchot Meyer. According to White House gate logs, the liquid conspiracy queen won the competition.

Again, Piccard's focus ranges far and wide from these important aspects of LSD use and movement through the conspiracy realities of JFK's life and death. He offers flashbacks and fast forwards through recent history that provide a chilling overview of a world gone wrong. *The Liquid Conspiracy* demonstrates how the potentially liberating energies of LSD, sex and even UFOs can be subverted by transnational spook agencies and control groups to enslave people into a hallucinogenic conspiracy nightmare.

Kenn Thomas
May 30, 1999

Kenn Thomas publishes the conspiracy magazine *Steamshovel Press. Steamshovel* costs $23 for a four issues subscription, at PO Box 23715, St. Louis, MO 63121. It can be reached on the web at www.umsl.edu/~skthoma. Mr. Thomas' other books include *Maury Island UFO* (IllumiNet), *Inside the Gemstone File, NAZA, NAZIS, & JFK,* (both Adventures Unlimited Press) and *The Octopus* (Feral House).

INTRODUCTION

THE MORE THINGS CHANGE...

On the morning of September 14, 1945, the members of several elite organizations met in Geneva to plot a sinister fate for our civilization. These groups had long controlled world events, but as of recent times had been ironically unable to command the technologies that they had developed. Their agenda was to institute a new methodology of world domination compatible with the modern industrialized planet.

Recent events lent an urgency to their collaboration. In the twenties and thirties, the bustling world economy had broken down. Poverty bred warfare and gave rise to charismatic dictators who were hardly manageable, let alone rational. Nations had been eliminated either by force, or with the stroke of a pen. Adolf Hitler marched over three continents, with his own vision of a New World Order. Four years after Hitler's fall, Soviet aggression remained unchecked. The United States had grown too large, too fast, and its once compliant political infrastructure was infiltrated by dangerous detractors and powerful idealists. Now more than ever, time was of the essence.

Technology had never advanced so quickly. Communications progressed rapidly, hence information disbursement was out of control—at least in the view of the men who had historically manipulated those communications. For over a decade millions of people had been glued to their radios and the sudden sheer number of broadcasts made the Truth more difficult to manipulate. Even more challenging, the Age of Television was just about to begin. Soon the people of the world would become mesmerized by the moving pictures blasting from this wonder appliance in their living rooms. The media and its messages were two steps ahead of the inflexible old time regime.

The arms race went unchecked, producing increasingly powerful weapons. Beginning in World War II, these weapons had been used to decimate human beings and their societies. But the truth was that the conspiracy didn't want mass casualties. They wanted unrelenting control, and the promise of continuing control.

Most threatening however, was the series of UFO mishaps which had by chance put coveted extraterrestrial alien technology into too many hands. Things had to change. And they had to be able to continue to change.

Those at the top of the pyramid sought a new means to carry out their destiny of total world domination. They needed a new plan, one which was infallible to threats unseen: the threats of the future. In Geneva 1945, this secret council of world power brokers met and agreed to formulate a new method of achieving world domination. This new plan must be able to evolve and adapt to the necessary conditions. From one moment to the next, the conspiracy would take on a new form dependent on the wishes of its masters. Only after a considerable passage of time was it possible for people who were not insiders in the conspiracy to determine the true nature of this ever mutating stratagem.

A *new* conspiracy for total world control was to be initiated, one which was fluid: *A Liquid Conspiracy.*

On the surface, the extent of the conspiracy seems enormous. The question arises— how could an agenda so diabolic, involving so many, remain secret? One must realize that the face of the conspiracy is deceptive if not completely illusory. The new plan of the conspiracy is highly aqueous: ever changing, ever distorting, and yet remaining within the complete control of its containers.

And what contains this revised sedition? Majestic 12? The Masonic Lodge? The Trilateral Commission? The New World Order? The Liquid Conspiracy's shifting face gives light to the sobering truth.

I have for years researched conspiracy related topics for various respected authors. I have established many contacts in the research world, both under my own name and various pseudonyms. These contacts have proved invaluable in my work. However, the network of information is littered with deception. Every lead must be considered suspect. It can take days, weeks, or months to verify data, if it can ever be verified. The road to discovery often ends in disappointment and the travel can become dangerous. At the same time, not many of us in the underground have met face to face. Letters, e-mail, and telephone conversations occur with regularity but one is never sure of another's agenda. So it was with extreme caution that I approached what was to become the source of my most important enlightenment.

Several months ago I received an e-mail from one of my frequent contacts. He told me of an elderly Englishman who had recently revealed to him "shattering information." He termed it "The Grand Unification Theory of the Conspiracy." I was very intrigued, but I was also busy with a handful of separate research projects and I sadly left his communique unanswered for weeks.

When I did reply, nearly a month later, my e-mail was returned with a user unknown error. In the following days I tried to reestablish contact. I telephoned mutual friends, and learned that my colleague had dropped out of touch. Not wanting to let paranoia get the best of me, I did well to assume the best and forget the matter entirely. It is not so unusual to lose touch with a researcher in the field of conspiracy, and the reasons are not always sinister.

A bit over one had week passed when I received a bizarre phone call on a Sunday afternoon. The call came in on my personal phone line, from which I do no business. The line was unlisted, and I expected only calls from family and close friends. The voice on the line was grave and undoubtedly English.

"Mr. Piccard," he addressed me, "we share a close friend. I understand you have been looking for him."

I confirmed this fact. I asked the caller for his name, and he declined to tell me—insisting that it was dangerous to speak it on the telephone. His fear was contagious and I felt my heart pounding. He sounded very serious, if not mad.

"I have little time left on Earth," he said. "I have a story to tell which will be the glue to all of your puzzle pieces. You must be discreet; no one can be told of this relationship, or harm may come to us both."

The Englishman went on to say that he had been hunted for the last few months by a Black-Ops division of the UN. Without further information, I had no idea whether to attribute his concerns to this real threat or to the paranoia which runs rampant in the conspiracy community. We arranged to meet in cyberspace with some special precautions.

Normally, I shy away from sensationalist claims but the circumstances and mystery of this man's telephone call piqued my curiosity and my fears. The time of our meeting arrived, and I logged on to the Internet. I went to a prearranged web page chat area. Before long, a sentence appeared upon my monitor.

Good morning. My secrets are about to become yours.

This seemed like an ominous way to begin a conversation, and I was hooked from the start.

The user introduced himself as Kilder, which I believe was a pseudonym. He had served in the RAF during World War II, and also as a clerk at the GCHQ (Government Communications Headquarters) in the late 1940s. It was during his time as a clerk that he had begun to gather his knowledge of the Liquid Conspiracy.

Simply out of boredom he had been secretly reading classified documents that he was charged with filing. Kilder was gifted with a photographic memory, and was able to quickly scan these papers and remain undetected. Kilder copied from his memory the details of what he read into his personal notebook.

The papers told the story of a secret organization which sought to consolidate the world's power into the hands of an elite few. Some of these men were well known, some were unknown. This group of would-be world kings was being monitored by a super-secret task force within the Ministry that did not even have an official name. Over the course of five years, the curious clerk would learn details of this elite group's existing web of dominion and its new terrifying ploy to bring the planet under its authority. He uncovered a conspiracy that seeks to master each man, woman, and child. Out of fear, he remained silent. Kilder had kept this information to himself until November 1963.

He had immigrated to the United States, having met and married an American woman. He became a CPA. When President Kennedy was gunned down in Dallas he at last revealed his knowledge to his young bride. She encouraged him to go to the press. He called newspapers and broadcasters and predictably was scoffed at. In 1964 he published a pamphlet under an assumed name. He became obsessed with exposing the conspiracy. Eventually this obsession drove away his closest friends and relatives. At last his wife abandoned him. Lonely and disillusioned, he gave up the fight.

For over thirty years he lived alone. He went back to his practice of accounting. It was not until he was recently diagnosed with terminal lung cancer that he again decided to share his knowledge.

Kilder and I spoke several more times before his illness got the better of him. He presented me with the leads that have become this book. He encouraged me to verify the data he supplied, and in many areas I have fleshed out his insights with information that I have personally gleaned over the years. When possible, all efforts have been made to validate the accuracy of the information within.

As Americans, we live in a deceptively serene environment. Most of us are unaware of the beast in our midst, and as a populace, we are essentially unarmed. Few of us possess any reasonable understanding of the techno-weaponry, known and unknown, that our government retains. And though we may enjoy and tout our second amendment right, we have become sitting ducks in the eyes of the conspiracy. There is no solution in arms. We will always be outgunned—they have ensured that.

When I have finished my presentation, it may seem that we face certain doom. It will appear to you that the dreary future that the New World Order is building is one which is irrefutable. When you discover the vastness of their influence and the disabling capability of their invention, you will feel insignificant.

In your frustration, I implore you to remember that violence is *their* tool. It is of no use to you. They have mastered that game. Confronting your oppressors with acts of terrorism or warfare will only serve their ends.

We, the people of the Earth, have but one defense, one strength. Information is our safeguard. The plans of the conspiracy are only certain when we have all surrendered. Share your knowledge with everyone who will listen to you. The strength of information grows when it is shared. Conversely, the vitality of a secret is dependent on the silence of its veil.

Why write this book? Why take the risk? Two reasons: One, my deep concern for the future quality of life for our children. Two, the more people that know of the truth, the safer that the knowing will become.

I received news of the Englishman's passing several weeks ago. Kilder was fated to bear witness to the conspiracy's maniacal design. Without his bravery and his cunning, this information may have never come to light. I have respected his wishes to withhold publication of *Liquid Conspiracy* until after his death. It is with gratitude and admiration that I dedicate this effort to him. I owe him much more.

—George Piccard, Feb 22nd 1999

CHAPTER ONE

BREAKFAST WITH THE KINGMAKERS

"Things are not always what they seem."
—Phaedrus

Geneva, Switzerland has long been home to dubious activity. The laws of the state are very liberal regarding financial privacy. Switzerland has an extensive and famous history of secret bank accounts. Perhaps it was because of this convenient air of permissiveness that the founders of the Liquid Conspiracy met regularly in Geneva.

Or perhaps it is the political neutrality of Switzerland that they found attractive. World leaders made Geneva their rendezvous point. It's always nice to be surrounded by friends.

For whatever the reason, on the morning of September 14th, 1945 the fate of the world was changed by a select few. These conspirators broke bread together in the elegant suite of a Geneva inn.

Until this meeting there had been a standing war between the two most powerful and most secret societies. Each had for centuries attempted to eliminate the other. This breakfast meeting marked the beginning of a truce between these groups and for the first time their evil intentions were united.

At this time a brief review of secret lodges may be in order. Since the dawn of civilization there have existed societies within societies wherein the members held significant power and influence.

21

Decisions regarding the direction of a society have often been made behind closed doors by men who were bonded in secrecy. These groups are almost always associated with occultic rituals, and in many instances their tradition includes contact with beings from outer space.

Just who are *they* anyhow? We have all heard of the "Illuminati" and the "Freemasons." Few of us know the significance of these lodges and how they have shaped the world in which we live. For the purpose of this book, I will pick up the story around the beginning of the 12th century.

The Knights Templar were a group of nine men, headed by a Frank, Hugues de Payens, and a Norman, Geoffroy de St. Omer. The Knights Templar were highly devout Christians who protected pilgrims en route to Jerusalem. They began with no monetary support or protection from the crown. When after a few months they approached King Baldwin I of Jerusalem, they were granted quarters at the site of the ancient Temple of Solomon.

There in the ruins of the Temple they discovered the remains of Hebrew writings which hinted at a drastically different history from that which had been reported by the Church. These remains turned out to be the reports of informants who were working for the pharisees during the time of Christ. They reported that Jesus had spouted blasphemy about the "God of Israel."

At this point it is extremely important that the reader keep an open mind. All of the secret history of the planet Earth hinges on this point. The point being that the life of Jesus Christ has quite probably been misreported. The writings that the Knights Templar possessed told that Christ preached that the God of Israel (the God of the Old Testament, "JAHWEH") was Satan. He berated the people of Israel for having made Satan their only God. Jesus had come into the world to fight this Devil and now it was believed by the Templars that the life of their savior had been falsified.

A benign quest began for the Knights. Bearing no animosity, in true Christian fashion, their purpose became to discover the true teachings of the Christ. In their pursuit they were urged to remain silent of their knowledge by their patron St. Bernard. Henceforth, this group held a secret.

More relevant information was gathered from a letter from the

Muslim Imam Ali. The author of this letter likened the disfiguring of the Gospels to revisions made to the Koran. Soon after, a Catharian document fell into the hands of the Knights Templar which alleged to be a remnant of the original Gospel of John. This New Testament Gospel was written by neither John the Apostle nor John of the Revelation, but rather by Marcion—a heretic who founded a purist Christian church at the end of the first century.

Marcion had met the Apostle. He taught according to the knowledge of Christ's life which was related through John.

In the unaltered Gospel, it is suggested Jesus taught that the Old Testament God was actually Satan in disguise. Also in this version of the Gospel, Jesus promised self-healing, so that only the goodwill of another person was necessary to salvation. The organization and temples of a church were irrelevant.

According to the Catharian John, Jesus preached that he was the Son of the God of Love. The Templar Knights adopted a battle cry "Long live the God of Holy Love" to express their devotion to the true Christ and their renunciation of the Old Testament God of vengeance. Evidence of the original Gospel of John may be revealed in the King James Version, John 8:44, where Jesus says, "You belong to your Father, the devil."

The Templar ranks grew though this information was further held secret by an order within the Order—the Marcionites. This secret order continued to uncover more and more of the true Gospels. These writings strengthened their view that the historic teachings of Jesus had been corrupted. And alongside these vicissitudes, the Templar Knights believed that the Old Testament was heretically included in the Christian Holy Bible.

These versions of Christ's teachings threatened many peoples. Jesus, according to the information that the Templars possessed, had asserted that the God of the Old Testament was a false god. Jesus preached that anyone could be saved who believed in him, the Son of the One True God. In the eyes of Christianity, everyone is welcome. Both the governments of Israel and Rome were jeopardized by this new credo, and both groups reacted to this threat accordingly.

After the crucifixion of Jesus, his disciples scattered about the Roman Empire, both to flee persecution and to relate the "good news." Meanwhile there was much debate about the details of

Christ's teachings. The written gospels passed through many hands, and the message of their authors was often sublimated for a message that was more acceptable to the temporal powers of the day. It was a prime opportunity to institute damage control. Clearly in the eyes of the Templars the true teachings of Jesus Christ had been altered if not lost.

We are all familiar with the Emperor Nero's intolerance for Christians, but he was just the tip of the iceberg. For three hundred years the early Christians suffered intermittent horrors. In early fourth century A.D., the Emperor Diocletian instituted what would be the last crackdown in which Christian scriptures were ordered to be burned and those persons failing to honor the pagan gods were mutilated and deported. Despite the efforts of Rome, the number of Christians in the empire continued to grow. By the time Constantine began to reunite Rome under one rule in 312 A.D., their numbers had become a significant force. According to Christian lore, on the eve of Constantine's final assault on Maxentius (ruler of Western Rome), Constantine dreamt that he was shown a sign by which he would find victory. This sign was the symbol that the persecuted Christians had recently adopted and, upon waking, Constantine had this symbol painted onto the shield of each soldier.

That day Maxentius suffered a fatal defeat at the new Emperor's hands. Constantine was a convert, though he was hardly devout in following the intentions of Jesus. He often had made religion a poor second to politics. It is important to understand that thousands of humans were butchered under his rule, before and after his "conversion." Regardless of his incongruity, Constantine took Christianity from a persecuted sect to a world religion.

One of the most profound happenings the history of the religion was the "World Council." Centuries after the crucifixion, there was great controversy between Christian sects as to the nature of Christ and his teachings. The emperor invited the heads of all of the various branches to the city of Nicaea to settle their differing opinions. For political convenience, Constantine sided with the Alexandrian view of Jesus as God Eternal, deifying Jesus as was common practice in Rome. Although none of the Gospels refer to Christ as God, a resolution was signed which named him thus. Those who signed became the modelers of the Roman Catholic

Church. Those who refused to sign were banished. The Church would come to be defined along lines far different from the teachings of Christ due to the political and traditional atmosphere at the time in the Empire.

An unfortunate side effect of stipulating Jesus Christ *God* was that it was further surmised that the Jews had killed this *God*. (It was not until very recently that Pope John Paul II officially pardoned the Jews for this act!) Henceforth another dark period for the Jews began. Like the Christians before, now the Jews of the Empire were persecuted. The Jewish people who continued to worship had to do so in secrecy.

The framers in the Nicene Council would go on to edit the contents of the New Testament. For whatever reasons, they purposefully neglected to include several existing Gospels. Furthermore, at an A.D. 523 council in Constantinople, all references to reincarnation made by Christ were deleted. And seemingly in paradox, the Old Testament was included alongside the New in the mandated Holy Bible. Though in the end the Empire may have been converted to Christianity, Rome itself molded the religion to suit its own ends.

By medieval times, Christianity was a drastically different organization from the one which was originated notably by a Jew—James, the brother of Christ. The Roman Empire eventually fell but the Church retained its power structure. During the Crusades, a number of secret "Christian" orders sprung up—some peace loving, some malevolent. These orders included the Teutonik Knights, the Knights of St. John, the Franciscans, the Dominicans, the Knights of Malta, and the aforementioned Knights Templar. Each group had a separate agenda and sought to control the destiny of the Church and the kingdoms of Europe. The stage was set for a massive conflict amongst the secret societies.

The Templars sought to restructure Europe based upon the revelations they held secret. Astonishingly, they wanted to eliminate the monarchies and set up Republics. They desired to set up a free economic system. Mostly, they yearned to replace the Catholic Church with an organization true to the original tenets of Christ.

The Templars were far ahead of their times. When their ambitions were made known the group fell out of favor and fell into hard times. The Vatican accused them of Satanic worship. Those that survived fled to the fringes of the empire. Some of them joined existing Masonic lodges in England. In 1314, the Grand Master of this group, Jacques de Molay, was burnt at the stake in Paris by order of Philippe IV (Note: today the Masons' Junior Order in the United States is named De Molay.)

While the Templars were disbanded the Knights of Malta rose to power. They succeeded in creating the most formidable military force in the Mediterranean. Their influence grew to control the monies of the Vatican. Now watch the conflict that develops here—the Ancient Masonic Orders had established strongholds in England. Perhaps the oldest of secret orders, the Illuminati, had secretly resurfaced in Germany. A main branch of the Illuminati, the Rosicrucians, were behind the push for the Reformation. Martin Luther was a Rosicrucian and he bore their seal when he nailed his thesis to the church door at Wittenberg. Francis Bacon was a Rosicrucian as well, and he was charged by the Crown with the coordination of the English King James Bible, first published in 1611. In fact, Bacon was the highest ranking Rosicrucian in all of England. Perhaps you can begin to see the amazing influence that these secret orders can have. The most widely used Bible in the world was essentially compiled by a man who was among the elite in a highly exclusive organization.

The soup gets thicker when it is learned that in 1770 Adam Weishaupt sought to attract the most successful and intelligent men in Europe to the Secret Order of the Bavarian Illuminati. He did this on behalf of a group called the Elders.

The Elders were soon guided by the Rothschilds, a thriving German banking family. In 1773 Mayer Amschel Rothschild held a secret meeting of the Elders in his Frankfurt home. At this meeting it was discussed how the order would gain complete control of the world's fortune. It is noteworthy that the Rothschilds held memberships in Freemason organizations. Within this elite circle was laid the foundation for a future union between the two orders.

By this time the monarchy of England had fallen under the influence of the Elders. Through a series of marriages the Stuarts were deposed from the throne and eventually replaced by the German House of Hanover which had direct ties to the Elders.

Under the rule of King William III, England became very indebted due to costly war with the Catholic French Monarchy. This debt conveniently forced England to borrow over a million pounds from (guess who) the Elders. Under the conditions of the loan, the Elders were permitted to set up the Bank of England.

The bank was further allowed to: set the gold standard, lend ten pounds for every single pound of gold deposited in the bank, and to consolidate the national debt and to raise that sum from the people by direct taxation. The money of England came under direct control of the secret order. But control of England's money was not enough. The Rothschilds saw it necessary to control the monies of every nation. Mayer Amschel's sons established banks not only in England, but in Germany, Austria, Italy, and France as well.

In 1782 a formal union was forged between the Freemasons and the Illuminati in a pact which brought together approximately three million members of various secret societies.

Now remember the Knights of Malta? You can see where the secret society battle lines were drawn. The Knights of Malta stood between the Elders and their plan to control the world's fortune. The Knights held the power in the Catholic states because they controlled the Catholic treasury. They desired to eliminate the Protestant rule so that they could reunite the Roman Catholic Empire.

The monarchies of Catholic states used the structure of the church to maintain their power. The hierarchy of the church made itself the mouthpiece of God. They alone stood between God and common man. By this means, the priesthood controlled the masses as well as the monarchies. Monarchs justified their reign as God-given. Therefore, they had no choice but to hold allegiance to the highest of holies. The Pope was King of Kings. And who put Popes into power?

During the time of Martin Luther's rebellion, Pope Leo X led the Church. Leo X was the son of Lorenzo Di Medici. Lorenzo was the head of a family of wealthy international bankers in Florence who operated under the direct authority of the Catholic treasury. Who was watching over the coffers at the treasury but the Knights of Malta.

The church regulated trade. Just a handful of families were granted permission to trade internationally, and all trade was performed under their authority.

The Elders and the orders which they controlled sought the end of Catholic rule for various reasons. The Templar-Masons desired to establish a "True" Christian church. Along with the Freemasons they looked for an end to absolutist monarchies and the establishment of Republics. The Elders secretly had planned to make opportune use of these groups against the resistance—the Knights of Malta.

I don't find it an appropriate use of space to reprint the clandestine writings for the purpose of this book. I have included references where you may find such documents which will both frighten and amaze you. I recommend highly that you read what is termed the New Testament of Satan (Illuminati). There you will see the plans of the conspirators laid out hundreds of years ago.

For hundreds of years, the Knights and the Elders both sought their own control of the planet. The Elders, Masons, and Templars had all been previously persecuted by Rome. Bitter resentment was at play.

The Rothschild empire, by means of its banks in all of Europe, has profited from the wars and the revolutions of the last three centuries. Take our country's war for independence as an example. The American Revolution was led by Masons. George Washington was a Mason, along with most of the signers of the Declaration of Independence. Don't forget that the Masons were under the control of the Elders through the Illuminati. The British Army which battled the Revolutionaries was composed entirely of mercenaries paid by Elder Bank of England money loaned to Great Britain.

One of the early casualties of the secret war was the French monarchy. The Freemasons helped to disseminate propaganda against the French aristocracy. France, still under Catholic rule, was next to fall. After a bloody and taxing revolution, a republic was instituted and the French adopted a constitution based largely on that of the United States. It is imperative that I mention the deceit behind the movement toward individual rights implied here. While certainly there are inherent evils in an absolute monarchy, and we may hold our human rights dear and treasured, there were ulterior motives for their arrival.

In Weishaupt's "New Testament of Satan," the document of ideology for the Illuminati, it is stated:

The introduction of the general and equal right to vote shall create the majority rule. By instilling the idea of self-determination the meaning of the family and its educational values shall be destroyed. By education based upon false tenets and mendacious teachings the youth shall be stultified, seduced and depraved.

The Illuminati describe Democracy as a tool toward their diabolical end. The text continues to describe a principle of control known as "ordo ab chao" which translates into "order from chaos." They use discord and conflicting ideology to divide and confuse. Where there is confusion there is susceptibility.

Leading up to our Civil War, it is alleged that the Rothschild family had representatives stir up tensions between the North and South. When war broke out, the Rothschild Banks loaned money to both sides. From London, Grant's troops were funded. From Paris, the Grays under General Lee found their funding. For the Rothschild clan, our bloodiest and most costly War was a win-win situation.

After the Union's victory, President Lincoln refused to pay the outlandish interest that had accumulated on the Rothschild debt. With the country cash poor, he petitioned Congress to print money to pay the Union soldiers. Could this have played a significant role in his assassination?

Lincoln's killer, John Wilkes Booth, was in contact with Vice President Andrew Johnson. The two had met in Tennessee, Johnson's home state. On the day of the assassination, just seven hours prior, Wilkes had dropped by the Washington Hotel— Johnson's residence. He left a note in Johnson's box after learning that neither the Vice President nor his secretary were in. The note read: "Don't wish to disturb you. Are you at home? J. Wilkes Booth."

Lincoln's widow Mary Todd Lincoln felt that Johnson was involved. In a letter to her friend Sally Orne, Mrs. Lincoln wrote "As sure, as you and I live, Johnson, had some hand, in all this." Andrew Johnson was a 32nd degree Mason.

In 1913 congress enacted the Federal Reserve Act which allowed for the establishment of a central U.S. bank. The number one shareholder in the Fed was the Rothschild Bank of London. Among the other founders were their representatives: Lazard Brothers Bank of Paris, the Warburg Bank of Hamburg, the Rockefeller's Chase Manhattan Bank in New York, and the Kuhn Loeb Bank in New York—all of these banks in turn headed by members of Masonic Lodges.

In opposition, Congressman Charles Lindbergh protested that the Federal Reserve Bank would function as "the invisible government." Through the Fed, the Masonic Lodge would go on to orchestrate every major political event in the United States through World War II, both beneficial and detrimental. With the banking power of greater Europe and the United States combined into an international central power, the Elders moved very close indeed to their debauched goal.

Let's take a quick look at how the Fed works. The United States Government borrows a sum from the Federal Reserve at a certain interest rate, often overpriced. The money doesn't necessarily exist (and now that there is no gold standard, the money is even more abstractly based). The Fed simply prints up cash when needed. The taxpayers pay the enormous interest on this debt yearly. The interest goes right into the pockets of the private bankers who own the Fed! Furthermore, pertaining to the National Debt, the Fed has liens against all of the property of the government. So essentially this handful of private bankers owns all of the public and private land in the country. Talk about power ...

In 1917 the Russian Leon Trotsky received financing for his Bolshevik rebels from Kuhn Loeb and Company Bank of New York. He trained these rebels in guerrilla warfare in New Jersey on a plot of land belonging to Rockefeller's Standard Oil Company. The rebels embarked for Russia with $20 million to proceed with their revolution. Soon thereafter emerged the Soviet Union, another fine product of the conspiracy.

Towards the end of the nineteenth century, Germany had begun to construct its empire. The lodges sensed a threat from the fatherland and were unable to stem the tide of expansionism. To counteract the threat, a number of treaties were entered into by England, France, and Russia to unite in case of a German war. Germany would become the battleground for the conspiratorial forces in the twentieth century.

With Germany so unstable and unpredictable, and with its

economy so impervious, it was decided by the international bankers that a World War was necessary to bring the nation under their control and to further bring the earth under one government. Public opinion was manipulated expertly by agents of the Illuminati, people like Thomas Herlons in France, Edward Baruch in the United States, Kelse Kezchen in Russia. All gifted men in the developing field of mind control. With previous treaties and strategic propaganda, World War I was an assassin's bullet away.

At the conclusion of the War to End All Wars, over fifty million had been killed. the blood ran green into the pockets of the international bankers and the huge loss of life justified a further centralization of power in the interest of peace. President Woodrow Wilson was the driving force behind the creation of the League of Nations, the first "one-world government." If the one-world government had succeeded, World War II would have never happened.

In 1921 the Council on Foreign Relations (CFR) emerged as the United States' brain trust to the League. The Council was founded at the direction of Cecil Rhodes' "Round Table" by members of the Skull and Bones order, a super-elite organization which has had members from the families of the Rockefellers, Vanderbilts, Harrimans, and Pilsburys, not to mention more recently George Bush. As a matter of fact, since its inception, the CFR claims every American President as a member prior to each President's election, with the only exception being Ronald Reagan. The innermost circle in the CFR is comprised exclusively of Skull and Bones members.

Unfortunately, the League's dominion did not extend to the super-secret power struggle of the conspiracy. Germany had been devastated by the war and both the Knights and the Illuminati capitalized on the crushed German peoples using the Allied victory as the basis to build up another World War. The international bankers had conquered most of the Western World's fortune. As long as there were taxes being collected to pay the interest on the national debts, the bankers continued to profit. But when the world plunged into an economic depression there was only one solution to save the bottom line.

While Wilson's League of Nations was certainly flawed, its demise was aided by those seeking a replay. A war of horrific

31

proportions was summoned up and created by the bankers and the Knights of Malta; however, not even the conspiracy could foretell how uncontrollable their monster would become. . .

Adolph Hitler was born on April 20th, 1889 in Austria. He was the son of a peasant girl and a minor customs official. He aspired to be an artist, but was rejected from art school on at least two occasions. He did not finish high school. He lived on an orphan's pension first, and then on the small amount of art that he sold. He was from an impoverished background and suffered from further poverty due to the first World War and its resulting impact. Hitler developed anti-Semitic and anti-democratic views from early on. Curiously, this most hated and evil man of history was a vegetarian. When he was a young man he joined the Bavarian Army, and was recognized as a dedicated soldier.

Out of the military, Adolph Hitler became active in the National Socialist German Workers Party. The NSDAP was an instrument of the Thule-Gesellschaft, an anti-Illuminati organization with a particular slant toward the occult, black magic, and the belief in the extraterrestrial origin of civilization.

The Thule had ties to the Ordo Templi Orientis, and Aleister Crowley's Golden Dawn. They had extensive knowledge of Masonic secrets, and of the network of international bankers. Hitler was privy to this knowledge and he was himself very involved in ritual magic when he entered the inner circle of this little-discussed secret society.

Thule believed that the Aryan race was the most ancient on the face of the planet. They were named after the capital city on the first Aryan continent which predated Atlantis and Lemuria. This first continent was settled by the Thule Aryans who were from outer space. They claimed the Aldebaran solar system, in the constellation Taurus, as their home. When the last ice age drowned the Aryan continent, the population split into two halves. One half founded Europe and the other went *into* the Earth where they lived and constructed an advanced civilization. The Thule further believe the world is hollow, and there exists a black sun in the center of the Earth which supports the subterraneans. The symbol used by the Thule-Gesellschaft was a counter-clockwise swastika. This bizarre order purported that the Aryan race was superior and above all others.

The Thule represent a moment when the conspirators' wires got crossed. At once the order was heavily influenced by surviving Knights Templar, via the Societas Templi Marcioni, and made it an imperative to eliminate the Catholic false church. The Thule thought Christ to be an Aryan. Also, the Thule sought to bring down the international bankers who had become the masters of war.

In 1933, with Hitler named chancellor, the Thule-Gesellschaft came to power in Germany. Many critics feared that the Nazi party would fall victim to corporate influence but that simply was not the case. There were desperate attempts to influence the dictator but Hitler instead made efficient use of the puppeteers.

Among the American financial supporters of the Third Reich were: the Harriman Bank (strongly allied with Skull and Bones), General Electric, General Motors, and Du Pont. The antagonist of the Second World War was built by big American money. American money was controlled by the Federal Reserve, which in turn was under the reign of the international bankers. The bankers, if you'll remember, were the inner circle at the top of the pyramid.

It was no coincidence that Italy (the seat of Rome) aligned with the Nazis. When Hitler began to roll over Europe and North Africa, the Roman powers realized that he was out to conquer the empire that the Illuminati had built. Hitler attracted the Italians with the promise of establishing a One-World Axis Government. But be sure, he had no intention of sharing the spoils of his victory.

Hitler even briefly expelled the Thule from Germany, asserting his role as supreme ruler. He had under his power the most threatening army the world had yet seen. He had systematically taken the minds and hearts of his countrymen. All of the Fatherland was prepared to reestablish Aryan supremacy at any cost. So while the international bankers looked forward to a long and profitable war, the very man that the conspiracy had built now stood poised to destroy them.

Both sides of the conspiracy pulled no punches in ousting their brainchild. The war machine was run to full tilt. It is now widely accepted that our Government knew of the Japanese plans to attack Pearl Harbor. On that day of infamy, America, the last hope of the Illuminati conspirators, was called to the rescue.

33

The consolidation of focus for the secret orders came at a high price. While they were looking the other way, the mice were at play.

The sheer numbers of innocents murdered through genocide by the Nazi regime are staggering. Frighteningly enough, they pale in comparison to the numbers slaughtered by Joseph Stalin, leader of the Soviet Union. While the world was fighting, the anti-Semite Stalin was using the bankers' money and American weaponry to solidify his "evil empire." The Illuminati were being handed their asses in their own game.

Technology progressed more rapidly than ever thanks to the arms race. Germany proved difficult to contend with in that race. The Thule-Nazis dangerously pushed the frontiers of science with genetic engineering, rocketry, nuclear energy, mind control, and anti-gravity. The spin-off technologies proved impossible to contain for the conspiracy. While they were scrambling to put asunder their baby dictator, powerful knowledge fell into the possession of the masses.

Italy, being liberated by the Allied Forces, switched sides in the war. This alone did not signify a pact between the two conspiratorial giants. It did, however, represent the beginning of a sinister new alliance. When the Knights of Malta and the Catholic Church realized that Hitler would eventually seek their elimination, it was realized that the only advantageous position was to fight the Nazis. Otherwise, Rome faced a certain doom of being wiped out by Hitler. Aligned with their mortal enemies, the Illuminati, the secret order of the Knights of Malta stood a chance of survival.

Hitler paid much attention to the Thule ideology. Prophecy was that at the dawn of the new age of Aquarius the subterraneans would be reunited with the surface Aryans. He sent expeditions to Antarctica, the Himalayas, the Andes, the Matto Grosso, and the Santa Catarina Mountains to find entrances to the subterranean world. His scientists were charged with building flying saucers allegedly using the lost ancient technology of the Aldebaran Aryans. Remember, according to Thule, the Aryans are extraterrestrials! They came here on spaceships tens of thousands of years ago! You may be laughing, but the passing time reveals more and more evidence to show that they may have been on to something.

Adolph had more to go on than the lore of Thule. Near the Black

Forest capital of Freiburg, in an incident much resembling Roswell, the Nazis are said to have recovered a UFO. According to the reports of men who were there, the Germans reverse engineered and built a number of different flying discs, but were unable to incorporate them as effective fighting machines in the war.

At the end of the war, it is widely held that Adolf Hitler fled to South America. He has never since been found. Is it possible that he may have found his portal to the subterranean world? We will take a further look at this later on.

When the allies took Germany they raced to claim Nazi scientists. The super-secret sciences that the Nazis had developed spread out into the world, much of it disbursed unchecked. Wilson's League of Nations had become the United Nations, but the atomic age made it increasingly difficult for the body to stem tensions. Stalin began incorporating eastern Europe into his dominion, and his Soviet Union was on its way to becoming a nuclear superpower. Perhaps not coincidentally, hundreds of UFO sightings and encounters were reported. The world's governments scrambled to silence the truth for the sake of keeping their own secrets secret, but the dam was bursting.

It is safe to say here that the conspirators had made quite a mess for themselves. After a long history of dominating the world, their rule had fallen into severe jeopardy. In light of the recent staggering events, something had to be done to insure that the earth would forever remain under the thumbs of the conspiracy.

I will tell you in no uncertain terms that on the morning of September 14, 1945 the destiny of our civilization was forever changed. A plan was drafted which would bring the whole world under one secret power. Who were the players at this high-stakes poker game? Some of the names will look familiar. Some of them will astound you.

From the intelligence reports we can derive that the Elders, through the Illuminati, had sent several emissaries to the Italian banking circle. After a series of negotiations, invitations were issued to bring together representatives from the Roman Catholic Church and the International Banking Community. At the breakfast in Geneva the Church was represented by Angelo Roncalli, the *nuncio* (ambassador) to Paris, who would at the age of 77 become Pope John

XXIII. Pope John XXIII summoned the Vatican II council, where the end of the Counter Reformation was declared. Also at the Vatican II council the Church issued official views about science, space, and the Communist threat.

The Knights of Malta, at this time an officially recognized sovereign power of the United Nations, were represented by Lorenzo Gescheratte from the House of Savoy.

The international banking syndicate sent Harold Goetz, a New York-born financier who would later become instrumental in establishing the International Monetary Fund. Also representing the Elders was the Canadian Yori Keppler, mentor to Zbigniew Brzezinski who went on to found the Trilateral Commission and become a National Security Advisor.

Also present at this caucus was Prescott Bush, father of George Bush and descendent of the royal line of King Henry III. Bush was a high initiate of the Freemasonic Lodge. Along with Bush, the American George Marshall (of the Marshall plan) was reportedly present.

The most interesting guest represented the wild card of the pack. The person was known only as Schaufeld. The British reports that the English clerk Kilder witnessed described Schaufeld as the representative of the "extraterrestrial authority." He was a member of an inner circle of the long-silent Rosicrucian order. He was present to formalize a mutually beneficial deal with the powers which had come to govern Earth in which information and technology were exchanged for continued permissiveness and cooperation among the conspirators.

In all, the number in attendance was twelve. The rest of the names have been lost in history.

As amazing as the following information may seem, I can only report the information that I have been given. In the light of recent events, it seems to hold true. The Knights, the Elders, and the aliens made a pact. The conspiracy—its character subtly changed with their recent collaboration—made its final plans for the coming One World Order. The dangerous union of the Freemasons, the Illuminati, the Templar Knights and the Roman Catholic Church, with the support of the Grey aliens, brought to an end a fifteen hundred year struggle. These rival groups came together to put aside their previous animosities and to forge an invincible power. They were forced into this unholy marriage because the beast they had built for the destruction of each other now moved to eliminate them.

The new conspiracy was an entity unto itself. Using ritual magic and technologies still never spoken of, the attendees initiated an incredible device. A poltergeist of sorts, an ever-evolving energy form which would transfer power inner-dimensionally, from thought to reality. This curse (and I use these terms with reservation, for there is no other terminology to describe it) would grow, mutate, and adapt to the desires of its masters. The *will* of the secret world government would come to manifest physically. Still, actual temporal involvement was absolutely required. But with the aid and intelligence of their psychic contraption, their desires faced no opposition in the realm of the feeble masses. As you read along please keep in mind the people who are calling the shots behind the scenes.

Eventually, the investigations of British Intelligence dismissed the affairs in Geneva as mischief and tomfoolery amongst the frivolous upper class. You will soon believe differently. The Breakfast with the Kingmakers in May of '45 may have gone unnoticed, but for the first time in the history of mankind every man, woman, and child would fall under the rule of one secret order ... The Liquid Conspiracy.

Sources:

Allen, Gary, *None Dare Call it Conspiracy*
Bush Book Chapter 5 [Online] Available:
    http:\\www.kmf.org/williams/bushbook/bush5.html
Dorsey, Herbert G. III, *The Secret History of the New World Order*
Leja, Hector, *Templar Prophecy*
LaJoulles, Gestrand, "Illuminati Origins," *Peoples Truth*
Smooth, Dan, *The Invisible Government*
Sutton, Anthony C., *America's Secret Establishment*
van Helsing, Jan, *Secret Societies and their Power in the 20th
    Century*, Ewertverlag

BOTTOM LEFT: General Reinhard Gehlen, seen here as commander of the Fremde Heere Ost (Foreign Armies East), Germany's most important intelligence organization on the eastern front. TOP: Gehlen at a 1943 FHO staff Christmas party, as the war was turning decisively against Nazi Germany. CENTER: Gehlen with Wilfried Strik-Strikfeldt (center, facing camera), Gehlen's liaison officer with Vlasov. Gehlen eventually became chief of West Germany's intelligence service, BND; Strik-Strikfeldt became a prominent leader of CIA-financed exile programs at Radio Liberation from Bolshevism, the precursor of today's Radio Liberty. BOTTOM RIGHT: Edwin Sibert, the U.S. Army's chief of intelligence in Europe at war's end, who recruited Gehlen in 1945 and protected the Gehlen Organization during its formative stages. The Org was "my baby," Sibert said.

TOP: Nazi Germany's wartime rocket chief Walter Dornberger (left), seen here with Wernher von Braun in 1944. Dornberger set the schedule by which 20,000 inmates at the Nordhausen concentration camp were worked to death. BOTTOM LEFT: Nordhausen camp shortly after liberation by U.S. troops in April 1945. BOTTOM RIGHT: Dornberger entered the United States under Project Paperclip and eventually emerged as a senior executive of the Bell Aerosystems Division of Textron. The photo here is from 1954.

Alleged photo from SS files of a Haunebu II in flight circa 1944. From the German book *Die Dunkle Seite Des Mondes (The Dark Side of the Moon)* by Brad Harris (1996, Pandora Books, Germany).

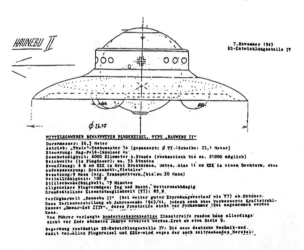

Alleged photocopy of SS plans for a Haunebu II being designed in 1943. From the German book *Die Dunkle Seite Des Mondes (The Dark Side of the Moon)* by Brad Harris (1996, Pandora Books, Germany).

CHAPTER TWO:

GERMAN GENIUS OUT OF CONTROL

As I have briefly mentioned, the scientists of Nazi Germany pushed the boundaries of scientific convention. Remember that Adolf Hitler considered the Germanic peoples to be descendants of extraterrestrials. Within his secret order, a technology had been purportedly preserved for many ages. This technology, known as "Vril" power, was either developed or rediscovered (depending on the Nazis' credibility) during the thirties and forties as an effort to produce superior aviation weaponry.

The Thules, the Aryan ancestors, flew to Earth from Aldebaran on "Vrilyas" or flying saucers. Under Nazi rule, the Germans attempted to replicate these ancient spaceships. Essentially the work began with the efforts of W. O. Schumann of the Technical University in Munich, a Thule-Gesellschaft member. During a forum he is quoted as saying:

> In everything we recognize two principles that determine the events: light and darkness, good and evil, creation and destruction—as in electricity we know plus and minus. It is always either-or. These two principles—the creative and the destructive—also determine our technical means. ...
>
> Everything destructive is of Satanic origin, everything creative is divine. ... Every technology based upon explosion or combustion has thus to be called Satanic. The coming new age will be an age of a new, positive,

divine technology!

Schumann worked feverishly on implosion power. Since explosion is a destructive force, its antithesis, implosion, must therefore be constructive. Certainly the Germans' science was heavily influenced by their fringe beliefs. Schumann invented a flying machine composed of three sub-discs which rotated separately using implosion chambers. He attempted to transfer the oscillating energy of the sub-discs into an electromagnetic field. Schumann theorized that at the correct frequency combination, a hyper-dimensional effect would ensue which would encapsulate the craft from gravity in a shell of antimatter. His efforts resulted in the development of the Vril Drive, but it is not known if his invention was a success.

According to Jonathan Barnes in his *Suppressed Technologies of the Conspiracy* the implosion concept had been known and kept as a guarded secret for centuries by the Templar Knights.

The scientist Victor Schauberger worked on a project that was stunningly similar to Schumann's. In June of 1934 he was invited by Adolph Hitler to join a Schumann-led project to build the first Nazi UFO. At the aircraft factory Arado in Brandenburg, this saucer made its one and only flight. Named the RF.-1 (the Runflugzeug 1) the ship rose from the ground to a height of over two hundred feet. It behaved in an unstable manner and it was determined that the guiding system was faulty. The pilot Lothar Waiz miraculously was able to land the RF.-1 and escape before the machine tore itself to shreds.

Before the end of 1934 the RF.-2 was ready. It had the first official Vril Drive and also a magnetic field impulse steering unit. The RF.-2 was a success. The machine had limitations though and wasn't sufficient as a fighter, but in 1941 the man-made UFO was used as a reconnaissance flyer in the Battle of Britain. The RF.-2 was photographed near Antarctica, probably en route to join the German discovery team aboard the cruiser *Atlantis*.

With the success of the RF.-2 the project was awarded its own permanent test site in Brandenberg. By the end of the next year the armed Vril-1 fighter was airborne. It was a single pilot aircraft which could reach speeds in excess of 7,000 miles per hour! It could also change direction instantly at any speed. A total of seventeen

Vril-1's were built.

A slightly more conventional project was the Vril-7. This project made use of a hybrid jet-propulsion/Schumann levitator. This airship met mixed success. It was sighted several times flying over Czechoslovakia and Austria, though fatal crashes were also alleged. The end goal of the Vril-7 project was to arm a saucer with atomic weapons and attack New York.

Within Hitler's SS there existed a group studying alternative energy. Their purpose was to rid Germany of its dependence on foreign oil. With the cooperation of Captain Hans Coler they assembled what was called the Thule Tachyonator Drive, making use of Schumman's Levitor and Coler's tachyon converter.

The Thule Tachyonator Drive was installed in Schumann's RF.-5. This was the program's crowning achievement. The RF.-5 was dubbed the "Haunebu I." It was one hundred feet across and required a crew of eight. It eventually reached speeds of 12,000 miles per hour. It was significant not least because of its armaments. It was equipped with two laser ray guns. There were revolving machine gun turrets, and the saucer was capable of transporting the crew into the upper atmosphere.

Later, the Haunebu II was constructed as the first spacefaring saucer. It is rumored that before the end of the war the Germans made ships large enough to hold hundreds of passengers.

Perhaps the most interesting note of the Nazi UFO program came in 1943 when Hitler instituted the Aldebaran Project. Two German psychics had supposedly received detailed instructions on how to reach the Aldebaran system and which planets were habitable by humans. Hitler ordered that Schumann's team build the Andromeda Device envisioned by the mediums. This hollow, blimp-shaped craft would create a dimensional channel and it would transport a Vril-7 inside itself and through that channel, faster than the speed of light, to the Aldebaran planets. Hitler himself made travel arrangements!

And let us not forget the foo-fighters, those mysterious luminescent spheres witnessed by Allied pilots. In November of 1944, the Allied pilots Henry Giblin and Walter Cleary encountered a large burning orange light near Speyer. It was flying at a speed of 250 mph and it was within a quarter mile above them. The plane's radar system began to malfunction. The pilots flew back to base immediately and filed an official report. The foo-fighters were again spotted by Pilots McFalls and Baker and then another report was issued. The Air Force Intelligence was forced to investigate the bizarre lights. The later report stated:

> At 0600 near Hagenau, at 10,000 feet altitude, two very bright lights climbed toward us from the ground. They leveled off and stayed on the tail of our plane. They were huge bright orange lights. They stayed there for two minutes. On my tail all the time. They were under perfect control [by operators on the ground]. Then they turned away from us, and the fire seemed to go out.

Soon after, the *American Legion Magazine* published several opinions of intelligence officers which suggested that the foo-fighters were pilotless remote control aircraft that were used by the Nazis to disturb and damage the radar systems of airplanes.

In January of 1945, the science editor of the Associated Press, Howard W. Blakeslee, gave a radio talk in which he reassured the public that the foo-fighters were simply St. Elmo's Fire—a natural phenomenon produced by electrostatic induction. This explanation did not satisfy witnesses of the foo-fighters, since the Allied pilots were well aware of the appearance of St. Elmo's Fire.

In fact, the Germans launched a number of fluorescent balloons to deceive their attackers. The lighted balloons would serve to lure away the escort fighters of bombing squads and at times caused whole formations to break up. Some of these balloons were used to lift decoy structures into the air to confuse the Allied radar. But did this scenario explain the sighting of the foo-fighters?

Under Project Feuerball, a device was built in 1944 in Oberammergau which operationally closely resembled the foo-fighter. The Luftwaffe completed research which produced an electrical apparatus that could interfere with an engine's performance. The device created an intense electromagnetic field. It was encased in a tortoise-shaped disc and powered by a turbojet engine. The fireball's purpose was to baffle a plane's radar and to disable its propulsion. As the front line moved itself toward Berlin, the fireballs were moved to underground bases.

The truth about the foo-fighters is difficult to come by. It should, however, serve to further demonstrate the Nazi's awesome grasp of developing technologies. Flying saucers, though certainly one of Hitler's obsessions, were but one shade in a rainbow of secret technologies advanced in wartime Germany. Another noteworthy endeavor of the Nazis was the research and development of gas and ray guns.

As the Allies occupied more and more of Germany, they came across documentation that the Nazis were producing *Kraftstrahlkanonen* or "projectile-less cannons." these were various experimental weapons which were capable of firing electrically charged gases.

According to French military reports, under production in the Hermann Goering Stahl Werke of Heerte, a Nazi-run war factory 30 miles from the secret Black Forest plants, was the *Windkanone*. The weapon was to designed to protect specific secondary objectives against low-flying airplanes where the use of conventional cannon was infeasible. The Windkanone was a thirty-five foot cast-iron tube with a three-foot diameter. In place of a normal breech, the cannon had a combustion chamber loaded with an ammonia hydrogen mixture. After being electrically fired, the subsequent gas explosion would create a terrific wind and was capable of displacing aircraft within a distance of 150 meters. Apparently, though, the displacement was so minor that the weapon was relegated to infantry use before being declared unusable. The Windkanone prototype was discovered by the American 12th Army Group in April of 1945 about eighty miles out of Berlin. Harmless in itself, it was the first in a series of clues to the extent of the Nazis' advanced weaponry program.

The American 12th Army also came upon another intriguing invention. This more frightening example of the gas cannon was called the *Himmelfeger*, or "skysweep." the weapon projected a gas ring that spun rapidly on its axis and created a sort of miniature cyclone, and had a much improved range of 3,400 meters. The cyclone functioned by throwing formations of planes off of their course.

Ironically, the Nazi Gas Cannon program may have encountered serious internal setbacks as they were careful to ensure that the gasses used were not poisonous—as gas warfare was specifically prohibited by international treaties. Adolf Hitler also personally detested gas chemical weapons and insisted on their proscription. Given that millions of Jews were gassed with cyanide in concentration camps, the Nazis' aversion to the use of poison gas in war seems contradictory, but nobody's going to accuse Hitler of being rational.

Perhaps it was a similarly logical aversion that led to the transfer of the SS power-ray program to the Japanese. Begun by Franz Leizschtgur of the Technische Akademi der Luftwaffe, the power-ray research led to several prototype laser beam weapons capable of injuring enemies at distances of 3,000 meters. The models were put into production at the experimental Zugspitztplatt factory. And though some were shipped to Brandenburg for use with the Haunebu I, the entire gas-ray gun program was apparently assumed by the Japanese.

According to the United States Military Analysis Division, the U.S. Strategic Bombing Survey reviewed Japanese research and development efforts on a "Death Ray." Though it seemingly never reached a stage of practical application, research was considered sufficiently promising to warrant the expenditure of two million yen on the program in the early 1940s. The Allied scientists concluded that the ray device could be developed and would be capable of injuring unshielded human beings at a distance of five to ten miles.

What wasn't apparent at the end of the war is very apparent now. With the aid of some very courageous research we can conclude that the Nazis had no intention of using a power ray as a weapon of physical injury. What the Nazis were truly researching was an ultimate weapon of domination. The Nazis had begun top—secret work on electromagnetic mind control.

The infamous Goebbels was gifted in the art of spin. The Third Reich is very well known for its mastery of propaganda, and its widespread use of propaganda techniques to influence the populace is often cited as proof of the dangers inherent with public manipulation. There was, however, a much more insidious undertaking in wartime Germany.

When in late 1944 Hitler realized his troops were close to final defeat, he ordered his commissioners to report on the most

46

promising technological developments which could be used to reclaim the tide of the war. At a hospital in Darmstadt, Hesse, research had been underway for some years on the effects of a specific electromagnetic device on wounded soldiers. According to the German Karl Hettig, a Nazi war crimes researcher, this machine drowned a subject in an EM field and interfered with the thought processes of the brain. The subject would become severely disoriented, so much so that motor functions suffered. Adolf Hitler apparently saw promise in the machine, as it saw further testing in the labor camps, disguised as a camera.

Hettig further relays that the machine never reached the front lines as a weapon. It seems there was difficulty in focusing its effects. Very often, the user himself reported disorientation.

There was also development of a brain implant in Nazi Germany, a forerunner of the type of devices later used by the American CIA in its MKULTRA mind control projects. Sketches of an apparatus which was designed to be inserted into the cerebellum were discovered by Russian Intelligence. It was apparently intended to bypass the victim's will-to-motion circuits and allow the direction of his physical movement by a controller. The device consisted of a series of three-pronged wires stemming from a vacuum tube component, all of which was to be inserted through a hole drilled into the back of the skull. From the component came a head brace culminating in an antenna. Several of these implants were tested on inmates at Dachau under the guidance of Hermann Becker-Freysing. The success of these studies is unknown, but may have laid important groundwork for sinister experiments to come.

The SS's inquiry into mind control wasn't limited to electromagnetic devices. Charles Perkins, a top U.S. industrial chemist, tells of a German plan for mass control:

> In the 1930s Hitler and the German Nazis envisioned a world to be dominated and controlled by the Nazi philosophy of pan-Germanism. ... The German chemists worked out a very ingenious and far-reaching plan of mass control which was submitted to and adopted by the German General Staff. This plan was to control the population of whole areas, reduce population by water

47

medication that would produce sterility in the women, and so on. In this scheme of mass control, sodium fluoride occupied a prominent place.

... In the rear occiput of the left lobe of the brain there is a small area of brain tissue that is responsible for the individual's power to resist domination. Repeated doses of infinitesimal amounts of fluorine will in time gradually reduce the individual's power to resist domination by slowly poisoning and narcotizing this area of brain tissue and make him submissive to the will of those who wish to govern him. ...

I was told of this entire scheme by a German chemist who was an official of the great Farben chemical industries and was also prominent in the Nazi movement at the time. I say this [with all of the] earnestness and sincerity of a scientist who has spent nearly 20 years' research into the chemistry, biochemistry, physiology and pathology of fluorine—any person who drinks artificially fluorinated water for a period of one year or more will never again be the same person, mentally or physically.

I.G. Farben was the industrial mainstay of the German war machine, and they employed some of the top German minds in their various endeavors. I.G. Farben researched the biophysical impact of fluoridated water on prisoners, then intentionally instituted the use of sodium fluoride to manipulate the German and German-occupied peoples. The use of fluoride was instrumental in Hitler's European dominance.

So how white are your teeth?

The historian G. Edward Griffin writes: "By the beginning of World War Two I.G. Farben had become the largest industrial corporation in Europe, the largest chemical company in the world, and part of the most gigantic and powerful cartel of all history."

Incidentally, on the Board of Directors of I.G. Farben appeared the names of Max and Paul Warburg, men who were also on the board of the U.S. Federal Reserve. Farben also had arrangements with Standard Oil Company and Alcoa. Farben was built with Rothschild money through the Union Bank, the Bank of Manhattan, and the National City Bank. The Nazis received direct financing from subsidiaries of ITT and General Electric. The conspiracy built the Third Reich but their monster took on a life of its own. It grew out of control. Nazi power came largely because of their war-induced technology. From the Blitzkrieg to the Vril-7, the unchecked scientific progression posed a danger to the unseen rulers. After the surrender of Germany there still remained a further threat. The very technology the Germans had developed was destined to fall into Stalin's lap. This technology was to become the true spoils of World War II.

Both the Americans and Russians instituted massive manhunts for the Nazi scientists. Russian intentions were well known. The Winston Churchill camp warned the world about the "Iron Curtain." The Germans were closer to inventing the A-bomb than anyone would today like to consider. The Illuminati had the United States under its thumb, but Stalin's influence was unbounded. It was seen as vital for the Allies to bring the German genius to the States.

Sources:

German Secret Weapons Sites [Online] Available:
    http:\\www.ufo.it/german/ger-link.htm
Gettig, Karl, interview conducted September 9, 1998
Perkins, Charles, a letter reprinted in *Contact*,January 31,1995
Vesco, Renato and David Hatcher Childress, *Man-Made UFOs 1944-1994: 50 Years of Suppression*, Adventures Unlimited Press, 1994
Vesco, Renato, *Intercept, UFO*

CHAPTER THREE

OPERATION PAPERCLIP

When World War II ended in 1945, Russian and American intelligence teams began to search throughout occupied Germany for military and scientific treasures. They sought out advanced aircraft and weapon design of the likes discussed in the previous chapter. The Americans and Russians were also highly interested in the often horrific Nazi medical studies. But the most precious spoils of all were the Nazi scientists who were behind the madness.

There is much intrigue surrounding the Third Reich. As horrible as their deeds were, there remains a certain dark fascination. According to Pauwels and Bergier, authors of *Morning of the Magicians*, "German technology, German science, and German organization" were "comparable if not superior to our own ..." Furthermore they state, "The great innovation of Nazi Germany was to mix *magic* with science and technology."

This alchemy would never have been accepted in the United States. Due to Hitler's occult affiliation with the Thules, and the association of many high-ranking Nazis with the occult orders, a separate inquiry into science flourished under the Nazi regime. The fact that this inquiry was successful lured the United States into a covert manhunt of gargantuan proportion. Under Operation Paperclip, U.S. military intelligence rounded up German scientists and SS intelligence officials.

President Truman authorized Paperclip in September of 1946 as a program to bring selected German scientists to work on America's behalf. He set forth the explicit condition, however, that no committed Nazis would be admitted to the United States. Apparently he was never aware that his directive had been violated.

State Department archives and the memoirs of officials from that era confirm the breach.

According to Clare Lasby's book *Operation Paperclip*, Defense Department agents "covered their designs with such secrecy that it bedeviled their own President; at Potsdam he denied their activities and undoubtedly enhanced Russian suspicion and distrust." It may be possible to wade through the historical sentiments and see that Paperclip was instrumental in building the Cold War.

The major obstacle to importing the Nazi scientists was that it was illegal. U.S. law explicitly prohibited Nazi officials from immigrating to America—and as many as three fourths of the scientists rounded up were committed Nazis!

The War Department's Joint Intelligence Objectives Agency (JIOA) was responsible for investigating the background of the scientists in question. In February of 1947 Director Bosquet Wev submitted the first set of scientists' dossiers to the State and Justice Department.

This first set of reports was damning. Sam Klaus, the State Department's representative on the JIOA board, labeled the first group of scientists reviewed "ardent Nazis." they were denied visas.

Upset with agency's decision Wev wrote a memo warning that, "The best interests of the United States have been subjugated to the efforts expended in beating a dead Nazi horse." He went on to claim that the return of these scientists to Germany would allow them to be exploited by America's enemies. He stated that this presented a "far greater security threat to this country than any former Nazi affiliations which they may have had or even any Nazi sympathies that they may still have."

On July 25, 1947, President Truman signed the National Security Act which founded the National Security Council and the Central Intelligence Agency. From the get-go the CIA was busy building its dubious reputation.

CIA director Allen Dulles was instrumental in the success of Paperclip. Under the command of Bosquet Wev, Dulles rewrote the dossiers of the Nazis to eliminate the incriminating evidence. For example, the original report on Wernher von Braun stated, "Subject is regarded as a potential security threat by the Military Governor." Von Braun was the technical director of the German Peenemunde rocket research center where the devastating V-2 rocket was developed. The revised background report, issued five months later, said, "No derogatory information is available on the subject." It also reported that Wernher von Braun was not a security threat to the United States.

At the Peenemunde Rocketry center, slave labor was used extensively, and discipline was severely enforced. As many as 100 slaves a day were executed by hanging, and their bodies were often left on display as an example. The SS was employed to manage the labor forces and acted under the orders of Wernher von Braun and General Walter Dornberger. Dornberger was convicted at Nuremberg of collaborating to murder 6,000 prisoners and he was sentenced to be hung. Von Braun refused to work in the Army rocketry unless Dornberger was released from captivity.

Dornberger received a full pardon from Commissioner John J. McCloy. After the war McCloy had pardoned 70,000 Nazis accused of War Crimes. McCloy was later employed as the president of Rockefeller's Chase Manhattan Bank and chairman of the Council on Foreign Relations. He also served on the Warren Commission.

It had been long decided that the Nazi scientists would be involved in the coming military and space programs of the United States. Wernher von Braun was first assigned to a U.S. Army program developing guided missiles. He later became the director of NASA's Marshall Space Flight Center. In the 50s and 60s he rose to celebrity status as an expert spokesman on the Walt Disney television show, "Disneyland." The Magic Kingdom employed the man who built the weapons that all but obliterated Great Britain! It has been said that if the V-2 rocket program had come into fruition, the missiles would have carried nuclear warheads to New York City. Nonetheless, in 1970 von Braun became NASA's associate administrator. Eventually he would head up the entire program.

Another Nazi welcomed into the United States was Major General Walter Schreiber. According to Linda Hunt, the popular conspiracy investigator, the U.S. military tribunal at Nuremberg learned that "Schreiber had assigned doctors to experiment on concentration camp prisoners and had made funds available for such experimentation." This evidence would have convicted the Major General if he had been made available for trial. The Soviets held him from 1945 to 1948. His security file made no mention of the evidence. Paperclip found work for him at the Air Force School of Medicine at Randolph Field in Texas. He worked there for a short while until a columnist's expose of his Nazi background forced the JIOA to arrange a visa and a job for Schreiber in Argentina at a U.S.-held company there. In 1952 he departed to Buenos Aires.

Kurt Blome was another high-ranking Nazi scientist. U.S. interrogators learned in 1945 that he had been involved in experimentation in 1943 with plague vaccines on concentration camp prisoners. He was tried at Nuremberg in 1947 on charges of practicing euthanasia, and conducting experiments on humans. Blome was interviewed at Camp David about biological warfare. He was hired in 1951 by the U.S. Army Chemical Corps to work on chemical warfare. His file failed to mention the Nuremberg trial.

There were thousands of other Nazis that were brought to America under the clandestine Operation Paperclip. It may well appear on the surface that the Paperclip story simply involves the U.S. government taking advantage of the research and researchers of the fallen Third Reich to strengthen their own political position, but that's what *they* want you to think. Alone, the idea of *our* country instituting a plan to employ these atrocious people is disillusioning, but the plot gets thicker.

According to information in my possession, the Liquid Conspiracy had an ulterior agenda. Many of Hitler's circle saw the end before it came. They fled the losing battle to secret locations around the globe. Their exact whereabouts were not known outside of SS intelligence circles, though it was suspected that the Nazis had secretly retreated to Antarctica.

Remember again that Hitler's regime held the belief that there exist holes in the Earth which lead into the subterranean world—or at least they wanted the world to think that they had believed that. Perhaps it was a cover for them to secretly set up military installations at these suspect sites. While intelligence reports of these expeditions led the world to dismiss their efforts, they had free reign to set up enormous secret bases. This could have occurred in a world without the aid of satellite technology.

The truth is that the Third Reich with a surviving Hitler could have very well been continuing their amazing technological progression with the aid of fugitive scientists who evaded the Allies and their programs like Paperclip. Though it sounds unlikely, we cannot dismiss the idea when credible research continues to discover evidence of the scenario.

German Author Jan von Helsing tells us in his book *Secret Societies and their Power in the 20th Century*:

> In 1938 a German expedition to the ANTARCTIC was made with the aircraft carrier Schwabenland (Swabia). 600,000 km^2 of an ice-free area with lakes and mountains were declared German territory, the "NEUSCHWABENLAND" (New Swabia). Whole fleets of submarines of the 21 and 23 series were later headed towards Neuschwabenland. Today about one hundred German submarines are still unaccounted for, some equipped with the Walter snorkel, a device that allowed them to stay submerged for several weeks, and it can be assumed that the fled to Neuschwabenland with the dismantled flying disks or at least the construction plans. Again it must be assumed that since the test flights had been very successful some so-called flying saucers have flown directly there at the end of the war.

Again, this may seem ridiculous. I'll ask you, though, to consider that the Germans did not act within the same bounds of reality that the modern Western world does today. As previously mentioned, the Germans sought to combine *magic* with science and technology. Simply put, they didn't think the same way we do today. As has been demonstrated, it was no stretch of their imagination to build 'flying saucers'; we have seen the photographs. Is it too much to assume that they may have devised a back-up plan where, in the event of their defeat, they could continue their apocalyptic endeavor?

Kilder learned of this plan from the MI-6 documentation that he saw. "It was known to the LC [liquid conspiracy] that the Nazis had retreated to South America and Antarctica and staged their final defeat," he told me in one of our interviews. The Germans went so far as to kill one of Hitler's doubles for the Allies to discover in Berlin. These remains were judged not to be those of Adolf Hitler, by comparing dental records. Hitler's body has never been discovered.

According to Kilder, the United States became the central focus of the Liquid Conspiracy plot. The financial infrastructure had long been under the Elders' control. The LC wanted the Nazi scientists and Nazi intelligence agents so that they could find and defeat the Third Reich—their only significant opposition—and control the dissemination of German knowledge.

In 1947 Admiral Byrd of the U.S. Navy led a mission to Antarctica. He took with him some 4,000 soldiers, a man-of-war, and a fully equipped aircraft carrier. It was publicly touted as an expedition, but considering the force that Byrd took with him, it looks a lot more like an invasion. Byrd was given eight months to complete his mission, but quit after eight weeks because of heavy aircraft losses.

In a statement to the press, Admiral Byrd is quoted as saying, "It is the bitter reality that in the case of a new war one had to expect attacks by planes that could fly from Pole to Pole." What could Byrd have been talking about, other than the super science UFOs of the Nazis?

In the video documentary *UFO Secrets of the Third Reich* it is reported that Admiral Byrd said that there was an advanced civilization in the hollow Earth that used its advanced technology together with the SS. Whether this is true or not will certainly be a subject for debate for a long time to come.

According to Jan Van Helsing, the Third Reich had assembled an army of 6,000,000 soldiers and 22,000 vrilyas for a planned final invasion of the Earth. But the Nazis were doomed from before the end of the War. The LC had knowledge of the German secret plan which they obtained from Allen Dulles.

Dulles, who during the war was the director of the OSS, was responsible for masterminding the SS absorption into the CIA. His brother John Foster Dulles (named Secretary of State under Eisenhower) was an attorney for the powerful Wall Street law firm Sullivan and Cromwell during the '30s and '40s, and chief U.S. contact for the I.G. Farben company. John was an avid supporter of the Nazis, beginning all of his correspondence with "Heil Hitler!" During World War II he arranged introductions for his brother Allen to the SS hierarchy, which culminated in a meeting with Adolf Hitler himself. Toward the end of the war, Allen Dulles struck a deal with

58

General Reinhard Gehlen to incorporate the SS into the American intelligence system. Gehlen was Hitler's chief intelligence officer.

Two months before Germany's surrender in 1945, Gehlen and his senior officers microfilmed the vast Nazi intelligence gathered on the USSR. The microfilm was packed in watertight steel drums and buried it in secret locations in the Austrian Alps. This information was gathered under Gehlen by the torture, interrogation and murder of nearly four million Russian prisoners. Gehlen made certain that he and his staff were captured by the advancing Americans, as planned in his gentlemen's agreement with Dulles. Gehlen used the microfilm as a bargaining chip in negotiations with the JIOA.

The CIA employed General Gehlen, and his staff, to institute a vast Soviet spy web. Gehlen called the shots from a walled compound in Bavaria. He was acting on the Third Reich's behalf, believing that the Nazis would infiltrate the political infrastructure of the U.S. through the CIA. They were using Dulles and Paperclip to secretly take over the United States!

Dulles established the private intelligence facility named the Gehlen Organization. As a formality, Gehlen was ordered not to hire any former SS or Gestapo members; however, he did. He went on to hire Emil Ausburg and Dr. Franz Six who had been part of mobile killing squads which killed Jews, intellectuals, and Soviet partisans whenever they were found. He also recruited William Krichbaum, senior Gestapo leader for southeastern Europe. Gehlen further employed the Gestapo chief of Paris, France.

With the cooperation of the CIA and the U.S. Army 970th Counter Intelligence Corps (of which Henry Kissinger was an agent) Gehlen set up "rat lines" to help Nazi war criminals out of Europe to avoid prosecution. With the institution of transit camps and by issuing phony passports, Gehlen aided the relocation of over 5,000 Nazis to places like Central and South America. There, mass murderers like Klaus Barbi (the butcher of Lyons) helped governments set up death squads in Chile, Argentina, El Salvador, and Nicaragua.

"It is often said [Allen] Dulles was a Nazi sympathizer. That couldn't be further from the truth," Kilder says. "Dulles worked for and was completely knowledgeable of the conspiracy." In a game of high stakes espionage Dulles let the Nazis spin their web, a web that led the LC right to the Nazi secret base.

When you ask people how many times nuclear weapons have been used, most will answer twice—in Hiroshima, and Nagasaki. The truth is that there was a third nuclear attack during the cold war era that has never been written of in the history books. In 1958 Admiral Byrd returned to Neuschwabenland with a larger allied naval force. They detonated two nuclear devices and destroyed the Antarctic secret base. This event is now public information, and verifiable through DOE records.

The atomic bombs spelled the end of the Third Reich's hope to conquer the world. With Gehlen's help, the CIA infiltrated Russian Intelligence (which was to become the KGB). After Stalin's death the Soviet Union became yet another dominion of the conspiracy. No Hitler, no Stalin, no more obstacles to the New World Order—thanks to the efforts of Dulles and the success of Project Paperclip.

"The CIA and the NSC are instruments of the LC. They are headed and staffed carefully with lodge brothers and confidants to the cause," Kilder told me. "Paperclip, Lusty, and MKULTRA. The CIA made the weapons for the coming one world government."

Sources:

Fris, Emerson, *The Fourth Reich and World War Three*, Third Eye Publications
Keith, Jim, *Casebook on Alternative 3*, Illuminet Press
Kilder, William, various interviews 1997-1998
Operation Paperclip casefile [Online] Available:
    http:\\www.marsweb.com/~watcher/nwonazi.htm
UFO Secrets of the Third Reich, UFO Video Inc.
Vankin, Jonathan, *Conspiracies, Cover-ups & Crimes: from Dallas to Waco*, Illuminet Press

Alleged photo from SS files of a Haunebu II in flight circa 1944. Note the Panzer tank canon mounted underneath the craft. From the German book *Die Dunkle Seite Des Mondes (The Dark Side of the Moon)* by Brad Harris (1996, Pandora Books, Germany).

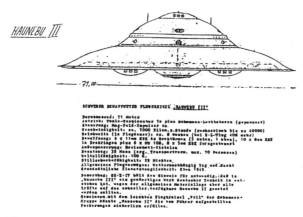

Alleged photocopy of SS plans for a Haunebu III being designed in 1945. From the German book *Die Dunkle Seite Des Mondes (The Dark Side of the Moon)* by Brad Harris (1996, Pandora Books, Germany).

Alleged photos from SS files of a Haunebu II in flight circa 1944. Note the Panzer tank canon mounted underneath the craft. From the German book *Die Dunkle Seite Des Mondes (The Dark Side of the Moon)* by Brad Harris (1996, Pandora Books, Germany).

CHAPTER FOUR

MIND CONTROL: SOURCE CODE FOR THE NEW WORLD ORDER

The control of human behavior has been pursued throughout history by various secret factions. From early legends of "spells" to their modern clinical counterpart "hypnosis," from information control to divine "revelations," there have long been efforts to manipulate the will of the people.

In the long-debated Protocols—which are an accurate assessment of secret control, whether or not they are actually a document of the Elders—a plan to control public opinion through the printed media is decided. Regarding "the future of the printing press" the Protocols have this to offer:

> Not a single announcement will reach the public without our control. Even now this is already being attained by us inasmuch as news items are received by a few agencies, in whose offices they are focused from all parts of the world. These agencies will then be already entirely ours and will give publicity only to what we dictate to them.
>
> The instrument of thought will become an educative means in the hands of our government, which no longer allow the mass of the nation to be led astray in by-ways

and fantasies about the blessings of progress.

The literature of Weishaupt's Illuminati reveals:

> The first secret of guiding people is the control of public opinion by sowing discord, doubt, and contradictory views until people can no longer find their way in this confusion and are convinced that it was better not to have a personal opinion in national law.
>
> The power of the personality has to be fought, as there is nothing more dangerous. If it is endowed with creative spiritual forces, it can affect more than millions of people.

The plans of the secret orders have been in effect for a number of years. Currently, the leading positions at the following news agencies are filled by members of the Council on Foreign Relations: Reuters, Associated Press, United Press, Wall Street Journal, New York Times, L.A. Times, Washington Post, ABC, NBC and CBS—to name a few.

As discussed earlier, the "Round Table" of Cecil Rhodes was instrumental in the formation of the CFR. There existed another group founded by the "Round Table" known as the Royal Institute for International Affairs. The RIIA was a brainchild of Cecil Rhodes, who wanted to extend British sovereignty over the globe—most of all he wanted to retake the "American Colonies." He is even once quoted as saying, "I would annex the planets if I could."

One of the main focuses of the RIIA was "social conditioning." In 1921 Major John Rawlings Reese, trained member of the RIIA, founded the Tavistock Institute for Human Relations in Great Britain. According to Jim Keith in *Mind Control, World Control*, Tavistock has been a major nexus for the world-wide psychological manipulation that has taken place over the last 50 years.

Reese dreamt of building a society in which "it is possible for any member of any social group to be treated without resort to legal means and if even if they do not desire such treatment." Tavistock practices what they call "societry," which is psychology on the planet as a whole.

In 1932 the German psychologist Kurt Lewin was named as director of Tavistock. Keith relays that Lewin instituted "research into mass brainwashing, applying the results of repeated trauma and torture in mind control to society at large." Lewin theorized that if a society as a whole were subjected to a sense of terror, then society would revert to a blank slate where control could easily be applied from the exterior.

At the conclusion of World War II, Reese suggested that "psychological shock troops" from Tavistock should infiltrate the populace and engineer the future direction of society.

The foundation represents an unabashed inquiry into psychological manipulation. Tavistock was founded by and for the conspiracy by men and groups who had direct ties to the international banking network and the Illuminati. The Tavistock institute relies wholly on large anonymous grants.

We have already learned about some of the Nazis' horrific pursuits in mind control. Portions of that research could claim earlier origins. Walter Rudolf Hess was Director of the Physiological Institute at Zurich from 1917 to 1931. There, he conducted several electric brain stimulation experiments. One such experiment included the insertion of fine electrically conductive wires into the brains of anesthetized cats. Given a mild shock, the cats went berserk.

The research of Hess, the Third Reich and Tavistock merely broke the ground. By the time the separate conspiratorial factions united themselves as the Liquid Conspiracy, mind control had already established itself as a prerequisite to global control.

When the LC eliminated its obstacles like the Nazis and Stalin it essentially obtained complete geopolitical control. But what about the cold war between the superpowers? "The cold war was a cover to maintain the arms race," Kilder explained to me. In the 1950s every aspect of the arms race was maintained by the conspiracy. Its purpose was to continue the expedient progression of technology. When all of this power rests in the hands of one order, it is but a matter of time before every last one of us becomes its slave.

Sources:

Coleman, Dr. John, *Conspirator's Hierarchy: the Story of the Committee of 300*, America West Publishers

Keith, Jim, *Mind Control, World Control*, Adventures Unlimited Press

Mind Control/Tavistock [Online] Available:
    http:\\www3.l0pht.com/pub/tezcat/Mind_Control/Tavistock.txt

van Helsing, Jan, *Secret Societies and their Power in the 20th Century*

Wolfe, L., "The Tavistock roots of the 'Aquarian Conspiracy,'" *Executive Intelligence Review*, January 12, 1996

Frank Olson, an early victim of MKULTRA.

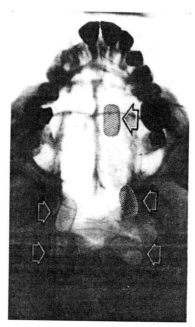

Above: X-Ray of an implant.

DESTRON/IDI

Injectable Transponder
TX1408L2
Large Size

Product Description:

The Injectable Transponder is a passive radio-frequency identification tag, designed to work in conjunction with a compatible radio-frequency ID reading system. The transponder consists of an electromagnetic coil, tuning capacitor, and microchip sealed in a cylindrical glass enclosure. The chip is pre-programmed with a unique ID code that cannot be altered; over 34 billion individual code numbers are available. When the transponder is activated by a low-frequency radio signal, it transmits the ID code to the reading system.

Although specifically designed for injecting in livestock, this transponder can be used for other animal and nonanimal applications.

Specifications:

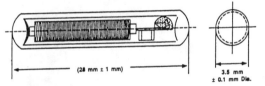

(28 mm ± 1 mm)

3.5 mm
± 0.1 mm Dia.

Dimensions (nominal): 28 mm by 3.5 mm (1.10" by 0.14")

Housing: Bio-compatible glass

Average weight: 0.77 g (0.027 ounces).

Temperature range: –40 to 70°C (–40 to 158°F), operating and storage

Read range with the Model HS5105L2 Mini-Portable Reader:
(In a benign noise environment with optimal orientation of transponder and scanner)

	Typical	Minimum
HS5105L2	33 cm (13")	30.5 cm (12")

Read speed: 3 meters per second

Vibration:
Sinusoidal; 1.5 mm (0.06") peak-to-peak, 10 to 80 Hz, 3 axis
Sinusoidal; 10 g peak-to-peak, 80 Hz to 2 kHz, 3 axis

Injector needle size: Approximately 7 gauge (Destron part # 445-0013-00/blunt tip and part # 445-0014-00/sharp tip).

Operating frequency: 125 kHz

Injectable Transponder
Suspiciously similar to those attributed to extra-terrestrials.

68

CHAPTER FIVE

LSD— WHERE THE TRIP BEGAN

"If you don't think it's amazing, go ahead and try it."
—Captain Al Hubbard

Al Hubbard was speaking about the infamous drug LSD, or d-Lysergic acid diethylamide, which he reportedly began experimenting with in 1951. Besides the altered perceptions of its users, it can be said that LSD has changed the perception of the world. No substance has so affected the direction of art, music and literature.

LSD is derived from the poisonous parasitic fungus ergot, which grows on rye. It was first synthesized at the Sandoz laboratories in Basle, Switzerland by Dr. Albert Hofmann. Its effects were supposedly not discovered until 1943.

Hofmann received notice in the developing biochemical field from his work at the University of Zurich. In 1929 he found employment in the Sandoz laboratory of Professor Arthur Stoll. Stoll had worked in a German medical research program in Berlin and Munich during World War I.

When in 1935 Hoffman's original program had been terminated, he asked Stoll for a new assignment and expressed an interest in

69

assuming Stoll's 1918-1927 work with ergot. Recent technological developments had made it possible to conclude Stoll's work of isolating molecular components of the fungus. In 1938, Hofmann produced LSD-25 with hopes of it being useful as a respiratory stimulant. It however did not arouse interest in the physicians or pharmacologists at Sandoz.

In his book *LSD My Problem Child*, Dr. Hoffman tells us that in the spring of 1943 the pharmacology department of Sandoz allowed him to repeat his LSD-25 synthesis. During the War, reopening the inquiry into an already researched chemical was unprecedented. In an otherwise thorough and technical effort, Hofmann mysteriously doesn't offer the reason behind the recreation of this apparently "uninteresting" chemical beyond his "presentiment."

During his work Dr. Hofmann accidentally ingested LSD-25. He theorized that it must have gotten on his fingertips during production. He wrote to his supervisor about the "Trip":

> Last Friday, April 16, 1943, I was forced to interrupt my work in the laboratory in the middle of the afternoon and proceed home, being affected by a remarkable restlessness, combined with a slight dizziness. At home I lay down and sank into a not unpleasant intoxicated-like condition, characterized by an extremely stimulated imagination. In a dreamlike state, with eyes closed (I found the daylight to be unpleasantly glaring), I perceived an uninterrupted stream of fantastic pictures, extraordinary shapes with intense, kaleidoscopic play of colors. After some two hours this condition faded away.

He soon after began self-testing of the drug, seeing research promise as it apparently induced a state similar to schizophrenia.

That is the story that has persisted for decades, but there are dots that need to be connected. Sandoz was owned by I.G. Farben which you'll remember as the chemical supergiant of the Third Reich. At the same time Hofmann was at Sandoz, Farben maintained a division that researched psychoactive agents. There is evidence suggesting that Hofmann was employed in this capacity.

Basle was situated about 200 miles from the Dachau Prison where

SS doctors were experimenting with a sizable mind control project involving brain implants and mescaline trials. Allen Dulles, at the time an agent of the OSS, was stationed at Basle.

Captain Al Hubbard, referred to by Timothy Leary as "a triple-agent," was recruited by Dulles into the OSS because of his communications expertise. Hubbard was a convicted rum-runner. His name looms large in the lore of LSD. As a CIA agent in the 1950s, he functioned as the primary supplier to LSD research programs at American institutions. He would be instrumental in popularizing the drug among the American youth and underground, but his motivation is often scrutinized. Whatever his agenda may have been, he was certainly privy to intelligence data and was often vocal. According to Al Hubbard, Hofmann's knowledge of LSD's effects came about several years prior than his recollection.

Why the disputed chronology? Is there something to hide?

If there is something to hide, it may lie in the early series of experiments with LSD conducted by Hofmann's supervisor Dr. Stoll. These tests were often conducted without the knowledge or permission of his patients. This pattern was unfortunately repeated on numerous occasions and resulted in the destruction of many lives. The conclusions of this study were published in a Swiss pharmacological journal.

In 1949 the drug was brought to the United States from Sandoz by Dr. Max Rinkel of Boston, Massachusetts. Rinkel was an immigrant from Hitler's Germany. Together with Dr. Robert Hyde, he founded the first American LSD research program at the Boston Psychopathic Institute, which was affiliated with Harvard University. The duo rationalized that if LSD could induce temporary schizophrenia, then research using the drug could lead to a cure.

Dr. Hyde was the first Westerner to use acid. He took a hit of 100 micrograms, half of Albert Hofmann's original dose. According to his co-workers, Hyde became antagonistic and insisted on making his rounds despite his dose. Hyde moved his research team to Providence in 1957 where he set up a center complete with pinball machines, dart board and bamboo bar stools—all with agency funds.

In May of 1950 the first article on LSD appeared in the *American Psychiatric Journal*. The drug's early public reputation was as a psychiatric cure-all, prescribed to remedy everything from alcoholism to marital struggle. It became a focal point of the anti-war movement. LSD redefined rock and roll music, and gave way to a body of fantastic literature. It may well have spawned the personal computer revolution as the developers were also LSD experimenters. But long before any of this was to occur, the newfound miracle psychoactive had a torrid affair with the Central Intelligence Agency.

Sources:

The Constantine Report No1 [Online] Available:
    http:\\www.pufori.org/const1.html
Hofmann, Albert, *LSD, My Problem Child*, translated by Jonathan Ott, McGraw Hill, 1980
Jeni Gale's LSD Timeline [Online] Available:
    http:\\www.rfttc.org/~dpearson/gale.html
The Psychedelic Library [Online] Available:
    http:\\www.druglibrary.org

Above: Two photos of Delgado's mind control implants.

Senator Robert F. Kennedy lying dead on the floor of the hotel kitchen. The clip-on tie of his body-guard Thane Cesar can be seen near his right hand.

AARC, Washington

Sirhan Sirhan is taken into custody immediately after the shooting.

CHAPTER SIX

PROJECT MKULTRA: CHICKEN FRIED WITH THE CIA

"Say what you want about the CIA,
but they sure had damn good acid."
–Abbie Hoffman

It is fashionable these days to look back at the 1950s as the Golden Era of America. Our heroes were Cowboy Movie Stars and Baseball Players. Our cities weren't littered with filth. Ideals were solid. Families were strong. From our modern day perspective, the 1950s look pretty good. But with the Liquid Conspiracy, as you are beginning to see, appearances are deceptive.

Under Eisenhower, the Dulles family came to control the fate of U.S. foreign policy. John Foster Dulles was named Secretary of State, sister Eleanor Lansing held a high position at the State Department, and brother Allen Welsh Dulles became the director of the CIA.

During a speech at Princeton University on April 10, 1953, the newly appointed CIA director lectured his alumni on "how sinister the battle for men's minds had become in Soviet hands." Dulles warned that the mind was a "malleable tool," and that the communists had secretly developed "brain perversion techniques."

75

Some methods were "so subtle and so abhorrent to our way of life that we have recoiled from facing up to them." Dulles elaborates:

> The minds of selected individuals who are subjected to such treatment ... are deprived of the ability to state their own thoughts. Parrot-like, the individuals so conditioned can merely repeat the thoughts which have been implanted in their minds by suggestion from outside. In effect the brain ... becomes a phonograph playing a disc put on the spindle by an outside genius over which is has no control.

On April 13, 1953 Allen Dulles authorized the MKULTRA program. This project would become famous for its unusual and inhumane tests on human subjects. Few programs would be so rife with secrecy as the projects collectively known as Ultra. CIA Inspector Lyman Kirpatrick wrote regarding the project:

> Precautions must be taken not only to protect operations from exposure to enemy forces but also to conceal these activities from the American public in general. The knowledge that the agency is engaging in unethical and illicit activities would have serious repercussions in political and diplomatic circles.

MKULTRA was an umbrella under which many "behavior modification" programs resided. It was an undertaking to centralize separate but related Defense Department projects and to definitively answer the question of whether or not a man could be completely controlled through the use of mind control. Every possible avenue was explored. The electromagnetic approach pioneered by the Nazis in Darmstadt was pursued, as well as implant technologies. Most notorious though, was the CIA's experimentation with LSD. Thousands of unsuspecting people were drugged with acid and other pharmaceuticals. Some died from the negative ramifications of their drug experience. Agents pushed the frontiers with various attempts to program individuals. The research is one of our nation's darkest memories.

The precursor to Ultra was a project first known as BLUEBIRD, a black budget operation begun in 1949 by the Office of Scientific Intelligence, under the authority of the JIOA. The purpose of the project, led by Morse Allen, was to produce an exploitable alteration of personality in prisoners of war and suspected spies. Agents were dispatched the world over to retrieve medicinals which might be of use to the program.

John Marks, author of *The Search for the Manchurian Candidate: the CIA and Mind Control*, writes that one of the aims of BLUEBIRD was "To investigate the possibility of control of an individual by application of special interrogation techniques." A thousand soldiers were dosed with LSD in the duration of the project.

Intelligence documents speak of the July 1950 experiments of using "advanced" techniques for the interrogation of suspected double-agents in North Korea.

The project underwent a name change in 1951 to become Project ARTICHOKE, and transferred to the Office of Security. Clearly the experiments must have shown promise. ARTICHOKE further developed the "advanced" techniques by inducing a state of trance in unwitting subjects, then producing a subsequent amnesia from a post-hypnotic suggestion. According to government literature, these early mind control projects were focused on the goals of both being able to retrieve information from foreign intelligence agents and on limiting the retrievable knowledge of our own agents. That's what they would have us believe. In 1953 that focus was about to change.

A study made by the United States Army Intelligence Command in 1952 reported that the Soviet Union had purchased a large quantity of LSD-25 from the Sandoz Company in 1951, which was reputed to be sufficient for 50 million doses. There is little if any information to confirm this. It seems more likely that the study was a cover to justify the depraved events to come.

In 1974 Project MKULTRA came to the attention of the public. By recent law the U.S. Senate became the overseer of the CIA. The Senate began an inquiry into some of the CIA's projects. In a memo, a select subcommittee had this to say about the project:

From its beginning in the early 1950s until its

termination in 1963, the program of surreptitious administration of LSD to unwitting non-volunteer human subjects demonstrates a failure of the CIA's leadership to pay adequate attention to the rights of individuals and to provide effective guidance to CIA employees. Though it was known that the testing was dangerous, the lives of subjects were placed in jeopardy and were ignored. ... Although it was clear that the laws of the United States were being violated, the testing continued.

MKULTRA was a top-secret, highly classified operation, run under the auspices of the little known Technical Services Staff. ULTRA's existence was only known by a handful of agents, although they involved numerous psychiatric and medical professions in these projects. According to Jay Stevens, author of *Storming Heaven, LSD and the American Dream*, the project was designed to operate outside of "normal channels" without the "usual arrangements." It was initially funded by diverted money before a front was set up in the Rockefeller-financed Josiah Macy, Jr. Foundation.

ULTRA was born at the insistence of CIA Directorate of Operations Richard Helms, who recommended that the agency expand is works into mind control. Richard Helms was the grandson of a former President of the Federal Reserve, connected very closely to the LC. In 1966 Helms ordered the destruction of all of the program files, though the program may have continued. Somehow select documentation managed to survive which detail some of ULTRA's ghastly endeavors.

Dr. Sidney Gottlieb led the project. Suffering from a physical handicap and a speech defect he had served as a Technical Services Division staff member. Gottlieb invented a cigarette lighter that emitted a poisonous gas, lipstick that would kill on contact, and a pocket spay for asthma sufferers that induced pneumonia. The CIA created the Society for the Investigation of Human Ecology to facilitate his work. There he developed poisons designed for use against Castro, Abdel Nasser, and other foreign leaders who were thought to be inimical to America's interests.

A 1955 memo outlined several of MKULTRA's goals (the following points are quoted directly):

- promote illogical thinking and impulsiveness to the point where the recipient would be discredited in public
- increase the efficiency of mentation and perception
- prevent or counteract the intoxicating effect of alcohol
- promote the intoxicating effect of alcohol
- produce the signs and symptoms of recognized diseases in a reversible way so that they may be used for malingering, etc.
- render the indication of hypnosis easier or otherwise enhance its usefulness
- enhance the ability of individuals to withstand privation, torture and coercion during interrogation and so-called 'brainwashing'
- produce amnesia for events preceding and during their use
- produc[e] shock and confusion over extended periods of time and capable of surreptitious use
- produce physical disablement such as paralysis of the legs, acute anemia, etc.
- produce 'pure' euphoria with no subsequent let-down
- alter personality structure in such a way that the tendency of the recipient to become dependent upon another person is enhanced
- cause mental confusion of such a type that the individual under its influence will find it difficult to maintain a fabrication under questioning
- lower the ambition and general working efficiency of men when administered in undetectable amounts
- promote weakness or distortion of the eyesight or hearing faculties, preferably without permanent effects.

This is just a sampling of what they were willing to write about!
During the early days of MKULTRA, Dr. Gottlieb and his staff began to make regular recreational use of LSD. They were enjoying

the psychedelic themselves, and made a sport of slipping the drug into each others' drinks. At a party in November of 1953, Gottlieb dosed the cocktail of Dr. Frank Olsen. Olsen fell into a state of deep depression and his associates took him to see one Dr. Harold Abramson. Abramson made a follow-up visit to Olsen's hotel room carrying with him a bottle of bourbon and a bottle of Nembutal, a bizarre antidote if there ever was one.

Olsen was scheduled to enter a sanitarium, Chestnut Lodge, where many of the psychiatrists were in the employ of the CIA. The night before his arrival, he was reported to have leapt through his tenth story window to his death. His body was exhumed in 1994 and it was determined that his skeletal fractures were more suggestive of homicide than suicide.

It is curious to ruminate that Olsen was himself a subject of an MKULTRA experiment. Some have speculated that he was about to blow the whistle on the whole project. Dr. Sidney Gottlieb and the involved members of his staff received only a verbal reprimand which never grazed their records.

Secrets are not so easy to keep when those who hold them are frying their brains. In his 1980 autobiography *Soon to be a Major Motion Picture*, the notorious '60s activist Abbie Hoffman describes how he first came upon LSD. A former college roommate had been recruited into the Army as a psychologist and worked on what Hoffman termed "secret LSD experiments." Hoffman quotes the psychologist as saying "... this is a secret government project. Only a few people on the base even know it's going on." The old friend supplied Hoffman with acid in envelopes postmarked from Maryland.

We can only assume that Hoffman's psychedelic benefactor was stationed at the Edgewood Arsenal in Maryland, where in 1955 the United States Army began testing EA-1729 (the army's designation for LSD) in conjunction with the CIA's MKULTRA. In all over 1,000 "volunteers" were involved, many of them unwittingly dosed. The purpose of the first series of tests was to evaluate the drug's effect on an individual's ability to act as a soldier.

Another round of testing began at Edgewood in 1958 where Army scientists analyzed the potential effects of LSD. Three phases of this program were described in the Senate Report:

1. LSD was administered surreptitiously at a simulated social reception to volunteer subjects who were unaware of the purpose or nature of the tests in which they were participating; 2. LSD was administered to volunteers who were subsequently polygraphed; and 3. LSD was administered to volunteers who were then confined to "isolation chambers."

The Edgewood Arsenal tests were known officially as Material Testing Program EA-1729. The supposed purpose behind these inhumane experiments was to validate the security training that U.S. agents received, and to see if their training held up in the face of unconventional interrogation. At the conclusion of the laboratory testing phase in 1960, the Army Assistant Chief of Staff for Intelligence authorized operational field testing of LSD. The field use of LSD was suggested by a lengthy staff study issued in 1959 aimed to discover the effectiveness of the drug on foreign operatives.

The first of these tests was conducted in Europe by an Army Special Purpose Team during the summer of 1961. Known as Project THIRD CHANCE these experiments involved ten subjects. All but one, a U.S. soldier accused of document theft, were suspected of being foreign intelligence agents. The subjects received LSD without their knowledge or consent.

The U.S. soldier displayed "severe paranoia" according to an Army report on his case. The same report also mentions, "This case demonstrated the ability to interrogate a subject profitably throughout a highly sustained and almost incapacitating reaction to EA-1729." In all, the success of THIRD CHANCE was moderate at best.

PROJECT DERBY HAT, a second series of tests, was conducted during the period from August to November of 1962. The purpose of DERBY HAT, administered in the Far East, was to "collect additional date on the utility of LSD in field interrogations, and to evaluate any different effects the drug may have on 'Orientals.'" One Asian agent suspected of espionage was given an unusually high dose of the drug which nearly rendered him comatose.

The Army's testing of LSD came to an end on April 10, 1963 at a debriefing session involving high ranking military officials. Though it was decided that more field testing of EA-1729 was necessary to establish its effectiveness, Deputy Army Assistant Chief of Staff General Leonard directed that no further testing be conducted.

Despite the notoriety of the Army's studies, many of the ULTRA projects were conducted through private hospitals and universities. There is some evidence suggesting that the CIA may have been involved with LSD research in America from the very beginning. Under the Freedom of Information Act hundreds of previously classified MKULTRA documents have been released. Among these, a memorandum from Dr. Gottlieb on "Sub Project 8" discusses LSD research at the Boston Psychopathic Hospital, and its secret funding. You'll remember from the previous chapter the work of doctors Rinkel and Hyde.

Gottlieb saw early on that drug experimentation on unwitting subjects was imperative to the project. He reviewed OSS files in a search for individuals to conduct such tests and he came upon the name of George Hunter White. White had been involved in the WW II hunt for a truth serum in which he supervised the testing of marijuana on unsuspecting persons. The director of the Federal Narcotics Bureau, Henry Anslinger, agreed to lend White to the CIA for the purposes of MKULTRA.

White set up shop in New York City's Greenwich Village at an apartment furnished with two-way mirrors and surveillance equipment. White posed as both a sailor and an artist. He lured his subjects back to his pad and slipped them LSD in their beverages, recording their reactions. Because the individuals frequently had an adverse reaction, White nicknamed the drug "Stormy."

In 1955 the CIA transferred White's base of operations to San Francisco and jestingly dubbed his subproject Operation Midnight Climax. White, under the alias of Morgan Hall, set up two apartments in the same fashion as his New York operation, but his tactics were more dubious. With CIA funds, White hired drug-addicted prostitutes at 100 dollars a night to bring their johns to his safehouses. These men were secretly dosed with LSD, sometimes in their drinks and sometimes through an aerosol device.

In Senate testimony the bizarre operation was revealed to the public. George White sat on a portable toilet behind a two-way mirror and observed the men and women engaging in sexual acts, all the while sipping gibsons.

Midnight Climax apparently got out of hand. White, still pursuing drug pushers by day, would invite his agents back to the apartments for some "R and R." The agents and White reportedly took advantage of the arrangements, using everything from hashish to LSD and even engaging in relations with the prostitutes. There were complaints from the neighbors about the half dressed men with shoulder holsters chasing women at all hours of the night.

George White, in a letter to Sidney Gottlieb, reminisces about his days in San Francisco: "Where else could a red-blooded American boy lie, kill, cheat, steal, rape and pillage with the sanction and blessing of the All-Highest?" White diaried the details of his career. He had received numerous checks from the CIA made to his alias and labeled "Stormy."

All of the madness caught up with White, who served with the CIA for a total of fourteen years. An associate who had helped to equip Midnight's safehouses stopped in on a social call to find the "roly-poly" narcotics officer slumped in front of a full length mirror. He had just polished off a half-gallon of gin. White picked up his pistol and fired wax slugs at his reflection.

Midnight Climax continued without interruption until 1963 when Inspector General John Earman stumbled upon the program during a routine inspection of CIA operations. Subsequently, Earman reprimanded Richard Helms for not briefing John McCone with regard to ULTRA. McCone was appointed by President Kennedy to replace Allen Dulles as the director of the agency. Helms had his own ideas about who was running the CIA.

In his 24-page report to McCone on the subject, Earman noted that the "concepts involved in manipulating human behavior are found by many within and outside the Agency to be disastrous and unethical." He reserved his sternest criticism for the San Francisco experiments, surmising that the validity of White's research was highly questionable because he was hardly a scientist and his motive to justify his own employment may have overridden the accuracy of his information. In his own words, Earman said that Midnight Climax placed "the rights and interests of U.S. citizens in jeopardy."

On November 29, 1963, one week after the assassination of President John F. Kennedy there occurred a meeting in the office of CIA Deputy Director Lt. General Marshall Carter. Sidney Gottlieb met with Richard Helms, Lyman Kirkpatrick, and the Inspector General of the CIA, J.S. Earman. The event was documented. These are some of the highlights (quoted directly):

- The main thrust of the discussion was the testing of certain drugs on unwitting U.S. citizens. Dr. Gottlieb gave a brief history of the MKULTRA program.
- Messrs. Gottlieb and (Deleted) argued for continuation of unwitting testing, using as the principal point that controlled testing cannot be depended upon for accurate results. General Carter, Kirkpatrick and I do not disagree with the point. We also accept the necessity for having a 'stable of drugs' on the shelf and the requirement for continued research and development of drugs—not only for possible operational use but also to give CIA insight on the state of the art in this field and in particular to alert us to what the opposition is, or might be expected to do, in the Research and Development of drugs.
- General Carter made it clear that he understood the necessity for research and development of all types of drugs, to include their testing, however, he was troubled by the 'unwitting aspect.' This led to a brief discussion on the possibility of unwitting tests on foreign nationals but according to (Deleted) this has been ruled out as a result of several conversations he recently had with Senior Chiefs of Station ... too dangerous and the lack of controlled facilities. ... If it is concluded by the DD/P that unwitting testing on American citizens must be continued to operationally prove out these drugs, it may become necessary to place this problem before the Director for a decision.

Earman insisted on the termination of Climax, but the San Francisco research continued until 1966 when White retired. Under

84

an "arrangement" with the Federal Narcotics Bureau a similar operation was instigated in Chicago.

At a study conducted at the Addiction Research Center of the U.S. Public Health Service in Lexington, Kentucky, Dr. Harris Isbell administered increasing daily doses of LSD to black prison inmates. Some of them were dosed for 77 days straight. The study required an "enormous" amount of the drug.

Operation BIG CITY, taking place in New York City, involved the use of a 1953 Mercury automobile with an extended tailpipe that was designed to exhaust an LSD gas into city traffic. BIG CITY also found its way underground when the project released LSD spray into the New York subway system.

The CIA's mind control research was by no means limited to LSD experimentation. In fact, the horror of MKULTRA was expansive. Sub Project 68, initiated in 1957, demonstrates a considerable disregard of morality on the government's behalf. The research was begun at the Allan Memorial Institute in Montreal, Canada and led by the powerful psychiatrist Dr. Cameron.

The CIA granted Cameron free reign. The CIA stated that "No agency staff shall contact, visit, or discuss the project with Dr. Cameron or his staff except under extreme circumstances." Sub-project 68 financed Cameron through a grant from the Human Ecology Fund, a CIA front operated from Cornell University Medical School in New York City.

Cameron's experiments ranged from cruel to sadistic. In what he termed "psychic driving" Cameron used repeated verbal commands to break the will of his patient. He equipped the Allan Hospital with pillow-speakers to program his patients while they slept. The good doctor even installed tiny speakers in football helmets which were locked on to his subjects' heads. Cameron theorized that with the use of repeated phrases and controlled states of consciousness, he could clear an individual's 'pattern' and return his mind to a state of infancy.

One of Dr. Cameron's procedures was to induce comas which lasted for up to a month, then to wake his subjects with electroconvulsive shocks. He also used the drug Sernyl to "block sensory input and produce underactivity," while psychic driving ensued for 20 to 30 days at a time. One of his patients was placed in a sensory deprivation chamber for 65 days before being extracted.

Cameron was a prestigious researcher. He served as president of the World Psychiatry Association and other major psychiatric organizations. Between 1957 and 1963 his empire of terror grew to include eight Montreal area hospitals, and connections to various university departments both in Canada and the U.S.. Sub Project 68 wasn't reserved for adults either, as children were unfortunately often involved. Lynne Moss-Sharman was just ten years old when the project began. The '68' survivor recollects:

> I believe I was taken to the U.S. in the 1950s (although living in Hamilton, Ontario and remembering most abuses in Canada)—taken to Colgate College, Hamilton, N.Y. (south of Syracuse) where Dr. Estabrooks was conducting his "research". Dr. Ewen Cameron was one of my abusers in the 1950s and I am in contact with survivors across Canada who describe brain washing experiments at various military bases in this country during the 50s, 60s, 70s.
>
> Some of the devices included helmets; rounded frames that were placed on child and adult victims/subjects' heads; a body contraption that included metal "bangles" around the neck, arms, torso and legs of children attached and suspended by wires—the child or adult was "directed" by somebody pressing buttons on something from across the room; there was a big chair and your wrists were strapped down—there were foot pedals, and the chair could be raised and lowered, or spun around; there were different sized containers for sensory deprivation and torture (?) because they would roll you up like a ball of string and put you in a box—another box had sides that compressed while you were inside; I was drugged from the neck down (so conscious) and electricity was applied to make my arms and legs move like a robot; all the children and adults had shaved heads and some were so thin they shouldn't have been alive—they were almost translucent they were so skinny; there was one place (I believe it was Colgate College)

that had different laboratory rooms—one was a funny colour of blue—the lighting—it always makes me think of dioramas at museums somehow; there was one man chained in place who had hands instead of feet, he was really skinny, and he was "frogman"; there was a boy who had monkey legs and feet—I call him monkey boy; over the years in therapy I have broken through layers of programming and told my therapist (when she quietly asked who was doing a certain technique to me) "for our navy, for our navy"—that was all I could say. I am now willing to talk to people about the alien involvement as well—there is so much it is very overwhelming.

There was also a bed-like container that was partially filled with water—they would pass electricity through it.

It is worth mentioning that those who were conducting the experiments may have indeed become experiments. Dr. John Lilly is one such case. Early in ULTRA he briefed the CIA on his research on mapping the brains of animals using electrodes at the National Institutes of Health. He would eventually abandon the field of study, deciding it was unethical. Lilly then mysteriously turned his attention to sensory deprivation chamber studies and continued to brief the CIA on his research. Much to the agency's chagrin, Lilly refused to let any of his material be classified. He would eventually leave the National Institutes of Health when it became obvious that he could not work without government interference.

Lilly, whose sensory deprivation notes formed the basis for the movie Altered States, began dosing himself with LSD in the chamber and came to believe he was in psychic contact with extraterrestrials at the 'Earth Coincidence Control Center.' He believed that the aliens were directing the events of his life, leading him to his amazing body of research on dolphins.

There is a wealth of lore surrounding CIA mind control. Separating fact from fiction, information from disinformation has served as a challenge to researchers and historians alike. There can be no doubt however that the agency, since its inception, has pursued the field vigorously. The question remains, what was the driving force behind ULTRA? Was it as the documents claim, an interrogative tool? A weapon of espionage? Or did *they* have something grander in mind?

There have been many lawsuits filed against the CIA for mind control research victims, and some reparations have been made. The victims' compensation was, nonetheless, a small price to pay for the dangerous knowledge unethically obtained by the Liquid Conspiracy during the experiments.

Sources:

Brecher, Edward M., "The Consumers Union Report on Licit and
    Illicit Drugs," *Consumer Reports Magazine*, 1972
CGIF's MKULTRA [Online] Available:
    http:\\www.chickenisgoodfood.com/mkultra.html
child mind control/torture [Online] Available:
    http:\\www.netti.fi/~makako/mind/cameron.txt
conspir [Online] Available:
    http:\\www.feist.com/~hemplady/conpir.html
Coup d'etat in America Database [Online] Available:
    http:\\www.weberman.com/htdocs/
Electromagnetic Warfare [Online] Available:
    http:\\www.trufax.org/reports2/emf-war.html
Leading Edge International Research Group [Online] Available:
    http:\\www.cco.net/~tru
The Lycaeum— Drug Archives [Online] Available:
    http:\\www.lycaeum.org/drugs/synthetics/acid.html
MKULTRA DOCS [Online] Available: http:\\www.parascope.com
"Project MKULTRA, the CIA's Program of Research in Behavioral
    Modification," Senate Select Committee on Intelligence report,
    United States Senate, 1977

An alien parade at Roswell, New Mexico.

The warning sign at Area 51 in Nevada.

CHAPTER SEVEN

1947:
THE YEAR
THE SKY FELL

In June of 1947 Harold Dahl, his son Charles, and two crewmen were on a sailing vessel in Puget Sound, Washington, near Maury Island. They were salvaging logs when they witnessed six doughnut shaped crafts hovering above the sound. The UFOs were about one hundred feet in diameter, and bright-metallic in appearance. Five of the saucers were circling the sixth, which was apparently in distress. There was an explosion from the center object and bits of debris resembling aluminum and cooled lava fell around Dahl, injuring his son and killing his pet dog.

The impaired saucer was seemingly "jump-started" by one of the circling units. The six crafts rose and disappeared into the sky.

Dahl reported the incident to his employer, Fred Crisman. Crisman, a reserve Pilot for the Air Corps and former OSS agent, had seen the debris on the shoreline and contacted Ray Palmer, the editor of *Fate* and *Amazing Stories* magazines. Ray Palmer sent $200 to Kenneth Arnold, a businessman researching UFO sightings in the Northwest, to investigate the matter. While Arnold was in the offices of *The Idaho Daily Statesman Newspaper*, bragging about the unusually large advance, the editor took notice. For whatever reason, the editor in turn contacted Air Force Intelligence.

The day after the incident, Fred Crisman collected some of the

91

debris. He witnessed one of the UFOs fly over while he was gathering the alien material. Kenneth Arnold claims to have seen nine of the same craft flying in formation near Mt. Rainier.

The Air Force sent two officers, Brown and Davidson from the Army Air Corps, to investigate. Kenneth Arnold showed the two intelligence officers some of the debris which had been collected, and the officers reported they recognized immediately that the residue was aluminum but did not say anything in front of Arnold, to prevent his embarrassment.

There is some evidence to suggest that Crisman may have switched the debris before giving it to Arnold. Dahl's original description, given to Arnold, of the residue from the explosion did not match the metal given to the Army. The Army made efforts to insure that they had obtained all of the pieces that Dahl, Crisman and Arnold may have had.

On the morning of June 24th, Dahl maintains that he was visited by a Man in Black. Dahl invited the man inside for breakfast. The man, who arrived in a large black car and wore a black suit, advised that engaging in conversations or further comment regarding the UFO incident would result in serious consequences to Dahl and his family. Dahl has since revealed that because of this visit, he decided he would later report the incident as a hoax.

On August 1st the B-25 carrying Brown, Davidson, the "switched" UFO debris, and relevant photographs, crashed. One of the plane's engines caught fire shortly after takeoff. The two enlisted pilots parachuted to safety while Brown and Davidson were killed.

Paul Lance, a reporter for the *Tacoma Times*, died of unknown causes two weeks after reporting on the B-25's crash. His article had suggested sabotage. He reportedly "lay on a slab in the morgue for about thirty-six hours while the pathologists apparently hemmed and hawed ..." The *Tacoma Times*, in operation for over 40 years, went out of business.

Ray Palmer, the editor who hired Kenneth Arnold, was fired. This despite his exemplary record and increased distribution of his magazine while he was at the editorial helm.

Arnold barely escaped death when his plane also fell victim to sabotage.

Following Dahl and Crisman's admission of a hoax, it was the recommendation of Lt. Col. Donald Springer that Crisman's commission be revoked. However, Crisman went on to fly during his thirty months' service in the Korean War.

According to researcher Kenn Thomas, Crisman had wired Kenneth Arnold several days prior to the Maury Island incident.

Crisman's name is important; he is a red-flag of the conspiracy. Remember Fred Crisman.

The Maury Island sightings are popularly dismissed as hoaxes, mostly due to the writing of Edward Ruppelt. Ruppelt was head of the Air Force's notorious Project Blue Book in 1951. He notes that there are conflicts in Dahl's initial reports, and also the film footage which was allegedly taken has either never been produced or is missing. The pieces of the Maury Island puzzle do not fit together well, but the hoax scenario doesn't make for a decent glue. Ruppelt later confessed that his research was conducted during an "era of confusion."

Why did so many people have to die for the Maury Island incident? Who was behind the cover-up? And what were they trying to cover up?

On the Fourth of July, less than two weeks after Dahl and his crew witnessed what was apparently a crippled spaceship receiving a jump-start, something mysterious crashed in the desert just outside of Roswell, New Mexico. As the reader is no doubt aware, no incident looms larger in UFO legend than Roswell. Volumes have been written regarding the event. The U.S. government has issued at least three different explanations since 1947. Whatever your feelings about Roswell are, it is critical that you realize it is relevant to the conspiracy to suppress information about UFOs. For it is my belief that whatever technology the LC did not receive from the Nazis, they recovered from the craft in the New Mexico desert.

The late Retired Colonel Philip J. Corso detailed the dissemination of technology recovered from the New Mexico crash in *The Day After Roswell*. According to Corso, we can thank our space-traveling brothers for: fiber optics, lasers, night vision goggles, computer microchips and even microwave ovens! These are just the things that filtered into the marketplace from Roswell. There was, however, a large portion of the recovered technology which never reached the average consumer.

In the early eighties, President Ronald Reagan made the Strategic Defense Initiative (SDI or Star Wars) an integral component of the United States' cold war research and development. Col. Corso illustrates that the President had knowledge of the 122 photos of the moon's surface indicating the presence of extraterrestrial settlement. The motivation of SDI, according to Corso and many other researchers, was to protect us from any possible alien invasion. SDI works using what is termed a "particle beam." And from where might this technology have arisen?

I am, however, not in the least convinced of Corso's assertion that SDI was to protect us from invaders at all, whether E.T. or Soviet. Given the track record of the United States, and that of the conspiracy, I would surmise these orbiting particle weapons were more likely intended to keep the masses in line.

Roswell is riddled with cover-up. There are cover-ups to cover the cover-ups. I don't have the time or resources available here to retell the tale. By watching any documentary or reading any number of popular works in the field, one is sure to get the gist of it. What I do have to offer here is something different.

You see, despite appearances, Roswell is a perfect example of the Liquid Conspiracy's operational procedures. Don't forget for one moment that every aspect of the incident was under their control. Every bit of information about that alien crash, from the sensational headlines to the hysteria to the recovered technology, was exploited to its full potential. The manuscript of the late Colonel Corso, who was once part of Operation Paperclip, may have been nothing more than an epitaph written by the conspiracy.

The web of the LC is infinite, and the strands of silk are rarely woven in a straight line. Every angle has been played against the other, the Army against the Air-Force, the military versus the citizens, the U.S. versus the USSR. The LC ultimately controls what is important, where it occurs, and what time it happens.

So what *did* crash at Roswell in 1947? The government has told us it was a flying saucer, then a weather balloon, then a high-altitude piloted spy-balloon test craft. Some have asserted that it must have been an atomic bomb, accidentally falling to the desert floor. There have even been theories advanced about Japanese *Fu-Go* balloons, which carried incendiary bombs to the United States via the Gulf

Stream. Many opinions regarding the matter have surfaced over the last fifty years. What you are about to read may surprise you; it did *me*.

The craft that hit the Earth that night was a spaceship. It wasn't a man-made vessel either. It was definitely extraterrestrial, although the owners of the craft didn't crash it. You don't fly across the galaxy only to crash in New Mexico. And no, we did not shoot it down either. Similarly, you don't circumnavigate the cosmos to get blasted from the sky by a planet of hairless apes. Yes, the craft that tumbled from the sky was a flying saucer, but we are the ones who crashed it.

The following is an excerpt from a letter passed to me from a fellow researcher:

> I have been interested in flying saucers since the 40's when I was a child. After the war my father was a serviceman in the U.S. Army. He was stationed at Wright Patterson and our family lived off-base nearby. I overheard conversations he made with my mother about a strange airplane at the base, I asked him what it looked like. He teased me that it was a spaceship. This was about the same time as Roswell. Later in that summer I answered our door one night and some men in military uniforms that my father did not know came inside. He said they were from Washington, and we couldn't talk about that 'spaceship' anymore.

After I received the letter, I made every effort to confirm its authenticity. I sent e-mail to my contacts seeking a validation. I received a message from a researcher who remembers speaking to a retired pilot. The pilot recalls that in 1947, several of his friends were training in a "crescent shaped" plane. The man told the researcher that "the machine was unlike anything he had ever seen," and it was "built with a strange metal."

Kilder briefly spoke to me about Roswell. He explained that the spaceship was probably a gift from the Marcabs, as a demonstration of "good will." For the LC, keeping the flying saucer a secret while trying to reverse-engineer it proved difficult. Secrets get destroyed in an attempt to fathom them and, paradoxically, sometimes the way to control a secret is to destroy it. So the LC had a Black-Ops group crash the ship in the desert in order to take full advantage of the minds of the military infrastructure. The military, despite all their denials, thought it was a UFO that they had recovered in the desert! The U.S. government has failed miserably at keeping that secret, which is exactly as the LC planned.

In 1947, following Maury Island and Roswell, sightings of UFOs became increasingly prevalent. The subsequent hysteria has been overwhelming. Today, everyone at least knows someone who has seen a UFO. And as you will read later in this book, there is evidence to suggest that many of these UFO encounters are part of a far-reaching CIA/Military Psy-Ops program.

This is how the Liquid Conspiracy works. It evolves to its environment. It sabotages parts of itself simply as a diversion. Its weaknesses become its strengths. At times, control can only come through chaos; "ordo ab chao." Perhaps you are beginning to see as I have, that a mind-boggling trap has been built in which *their grasp* simultaneously holds and eludes us.

Sources:

Brookesmith, Peter, *UFO: the Complete Sightings*, Barnes & Noble, 1995
Corso, Col. Philip J. and William J. Birnes, *The Day After Roswell*, Simon and Schuster, 1998
Kanon, Gregory M., *The Great UFO Hoax: the Final Solution to the UFO Mystery*, Galde Press, 1996
LURKING IN thE SHADOWS—June [Online] Available: http:\\www.speakeasy.org/~davepa/shadjun2.html
Maury Island [Online] Available: http:\\www.ntdwwaab.compuserve.com/homepages/AndyPage/maury.html
P files database: Maury Island [Online] Available: http:\\www.home.pacific.net.sg/~kmlow/pmfb01.html

Alleged photos from SS files of a Haunebu II in flight circa 1944. Note the Panzer tank canon mounted underneath the craft. From the German book *Die Dunkle Seite Des Mondes (The Dark Side of the Moon)* by Brad Harris (1996, Pandora Books, Germany).

A Russian satellite photo of Area 51 in Nevada.

CHAPTER EIGHT

AREA 51

"One of those you-can't-get-there-from-here places."
—Gary Powers, U-2 Spy Plane pilot

"It basically gets down to there are some assets
they don't want people to see."
—representative for Area 51

"You're not going to get anyone to talk about it. Groom Lake is
probably a secret test facility and I don't have a need to know that,
so I don't know about that."
—Air Force Major Monica Aloisiom

Area 51 is a top-secret military base located at Groom Lake in
southern Nevada. This base has been known to be a testing ground
for 'black budget' aircraft. The site was first selected in the 1950s, to
test the U-2 spy plane because of its remoteness. Being located on a
dry lake bed also makes it an ideal airbase.

The base lies inside the territory described as the Nevada Test
Site, which includes Nellis Air Force Test Range. Area 51 is
approximately 125 miles north-northwest of Las Vegas. The entire
airspace is under the strictest control possible, with no ceiling limit to
that restriction. All air traffic, civilian, commercial, and military,
must receive special clearance to enter it.

The ground level security for the area is provided by Wackenhut
Special Securities Division, part of the Wackenhut Corporation
which has an exclusive contract with the United States Department
of Energy to guard a number of top-secret installations.

The perimeter is patrolled by the camo-dudes—Wackenhut
Security who wear camouflage fatigues that have no identifying

insignia whatsoever. The camo-dudes drive white jeeps with U.S. Government license plates. They intercept anybody who gets too close the borders of Area 51. Trespassers are arrested and handed over to the Lincoln County Sheriff, where they are usually fined $600 and released.

There are also tiny remote-controlled vehicle sensors which patrol the area around Area 51, as well as automated infrared computerized telescopic sensors, making an uninvited entrance nearly impossible. Someone is very interested in hiding something at Groom Lake...

In the 1940s and 1950s, the Groom Lake area was mined by the family of Dan Sheahan. Their mine was damaged by atomic blasts from the nuclear test site. The Sheahans claimed that their horses were killed by radioactive fallout, after suffering from huge open sores.

Shockingly, in the summer of 1954, Air Force pilots flying from the Las Vegas Gunnery Range attacked the mining operation.

"Buildings have been struck by bullets, several people have narrowly escaped being killed and some pilots have even gone so far as to dive down and strafe our workings," Dan Sheahan wrote in a July 7, 1954 letter to then Nevada Governor Charles Russel. In 1958, the Air Force bought out the Sheahans to begin testing the U-2 spy plane.

Gary Powers, the U-2 pilot who spent two years in a Soviet prison after being captured when his plane went down over Russia, wrote in his book *Operation Overflight* that the CIA operated Area 51 and that it went by the name "Watertown Strip" or simply "The Ranch." It is also known as "Dreamland."

Since a 1989 Las Vegas television broadcast of an interview with Bob Lazar, who claimed to have been engaged as a scientist in reverse-engineering a flying saucer just south of Area 51, the secret airbase has been a symbol of the U.S. government UFO cover-up.

The Government refuses to officially recognize that the base exists, though recent legal motions have at least verified their knowledge of it. The *Wall Street Journal* reported the story of Robert Frost, a sheet-metal worker who had been contracted to work at the top-secret base. His wife, Helen, tells of how he came home from the job with "flaming red skin" that soon began to peel off of his face.

"He was a pretty tough guy," she recalls, "but he burst through the door yelling in fear. Every hour, I'd have to take a washcloth and take off some more skin."

Helen Frost, along with another widow and four former civilian workers, sued the Defense Department for burning highly toxic classified materials in open pits. They alleged that the exposure to toxic fumes caused health problems ranging from skin lesions to cancer. The plaintiffs merely sought information to facilitate medical treatment and help with medical bills. They did not seek a judgment for monetary award.

For several months after the filing of the suit, the lawyers for the government refused to acknowledge the existence or name of the base. The government eventually responded by asking U.S. District Judge Philip Pro to dismiss the lawsuit citing that any disclosure regarding Area 51 would pose a serious threat to national security.

The government lawyers, in a shrewd defensive move, retroactively classified relevant documents, preventing the workers from using them as evidence.

The government takes protecting the secrecy of this base very seriously, and this effort extends to the highest levels.

The government disclosed that in the spring of 1995, the Environmental Protection Agency began inspecting Area 51. There are inspection reports made by the EPA, required to be public record, which the workers requested as evidence in their case. The government's lawyers cited national security privilege, but Judge Pro required an order of exemption from the President.

In Presidential Determination number 95-45, President William Jefferson Clinton ordered that Area 51 be exempted from any disclosure. The President indicated that it was of "paramount interest" to grant the exemption.

In the end, Judge Philip Pro dismissed the suit filed by the workers, nonetheless public interest in the mystery surrounding Area 51 continues to grow.

Network television has shown an interest in Dreamland as well. On April 20th of 1992, NBC broadcast footage, filmed with the aid of night-vision, which showed an amazing craft in flight. The UFO flew vertically and then made a right angle turn, defying aerodynamic convention.

In the same month, ABC ran a report on *World News Tonight*. Reporter Jimmy Walker was accompanied by Glenn Campbell, publisher of an Area 51 magazine called *The Desert Rat*. Walker was reporting from the roadside near the perimeter of the base while Campbell was monitoring a scanner. The reporter pointed out an electronic sensor hidden in the sagebrush.

Campbell, from listening to the scanner, discovered that the

101

reporting team had crossed one of the sensors. A white jeep drove by after ten minutes, and then a helicopter flew close to inspect the ABC crew. Shortly after the group had finished the report, a deputy sheriff drove up and informed the media group that he was investigating the possibility of a criminal offense, one which he couldn't name on camera.

To photograph the secret airbase is a violation of the Espionage Act, and though ABC did not photograph the base, they were detained for two hours by the local law officials. Their equipment and footage were confiscated by the Air Force, and not returned until five days later.

What is the conspiracy using Area 51 for? What is it about the location that must be so desperately kept secret? Certainly the government has gone through a great deal of trouble to keep the base's use a secret, touting national security. But where were our national security concerns while Chinese spies recently stole nuclear secrets from Los Alamos? If nuclear secrets are of less priority, what secrets are hiding at Groom Lake?

Researchers have unearthed classified documentation of Project Aquarius, and perhaps part of the answer resides in those documents. Begun after a saucer crash in 1972, Aquarius involves taking E.T.s to a 'base in southern Nevada.' The National Security Administration (NSA) admits that they have a project Aquarius, but denies it has anything to do with aliens. This despite numerous references to the project from Air Force officials.

The consensus of UFO researchers is that both extraterrestrial spacecraft and alien bodies are being stored at Area 51, and specifically at a location called "Hangar 18.". A declassified/reclassified government-issued security manual confirms that Hangar 18 does indeed exist. Ironically, the same designation is given to the 'blue room' at Wright Patterson Air Force Base in Ohio, where it has been alleged that a UFO and alien bodies may have also been stored.

A number of individuals who claim to have worked for the government have come forward to give their accounts of flying saucers and aliens in Hangar 18. Most of these people have concealed their identities for fear of retaliation. Even considering the problems with anonymity, the sheer number of reports of UFO activity at Area 51 which coincide with one another verify that the base is a hotbed of E.T. activity.

There is even a video taped interrogation of an 'alien' who is named Jarod. The interrogation was filmed deep underground at Area 51, and the footage was smuggled out by a man named 'Victor.' The tape has been heavily scrutinized by believers and skeptics alike, though the jury is still out in terms of whether the footage is actual or not.

By the estimate of Ufologists, Area 51 may well be an information exchange center, where the conspiracy receives alien technology in return for its cooperation with, or tolerance of, alien experimentation on abductees. This would do well to explain the strange lights in the night sky often appearing above Groom Lake.

These concepts may be difficult to embrace, and it is a current trend amongst the conspiracy researchers to dismiss entirely UFO and E.T. scenarios, but eyewitness accounts cannot be ignored. If we dismissed every unlikely scenario, we would be left with one thing: the apparent world which the conspiracy has designed for us. Much of the conspiracy seems improbable, and that's exactly how they prefer it.

I implore the reader to consider the possibility that aliens indeed are visiting Area 51, and that the secret government is receiving advanced technology from them. There are too many witnesses who have risked too much for this to be false. And though there may be volumes of disinformation regarding the subject, we cannot allow their deliberate deceit to inhibit the inquiry. Remember that one strategy for discrediting actual facts or events is to fabricate facts and events that are obviously hoaxes, thus casting doubt on the actual.

There are other strange things occurring in the Nevada desert. Often mistaken as UFOs are sightings of the top-secret Aurora Project. According to mystery aircraft researcher Adrian E. Mann, the Aurora is a hypersonic stealth airplane capable of speeds in excess of Mach 6. The project is run by Lockheed Martin's Skunkworks division operating out of Area 51. Geologists in Southern California have suspected Aurora of causing unexplained 'airquakes,' since seismic activity with an aboveground origin has been recorded. Coincidentally, *donut vapor trails,* characteristic of the Aurora pulse engine system, appear across the sky.

Where Dreamland lore is present, be sure that aliens are not far off. Abductee Net of Canada claims that the Aurora is often mistaken for a UFO because of its unusual triangular shape. The witnesses may be close to the mark, as the Aurora is rumored to make use of extraterrestrial technology.

Intelligence researcher Norio Hayakawa places Area 51 as one of several in a network of secret bases where the military is developing advanced biogenetic technology in underground bunkers. Norio also tells of a Black-Ops project named COM-12 which is conducting mind control experiments at the base, involving RHIC-EDOM (Radio Hypnotic Intra-Cerebral Electronic Dissolution of Memory).

Former COM-12 member Michael Younger came out of the covert closet in the early part of this decade to report on what he knows of secret government projects. He confirms Hayakawa's statements. Having worked for some time at Groom Lake, Younger has revealed that Nazi forces within American Intelligence have been abducting some 75,000 children each year and with the aid of drugs and RHIC-EDOM, turning them into mind controlled slaves. An impossible scenario? Unfortunately, it is difficult to verify any information regarding the base, due in large part because it doesn't technically exist.

Since 1989, UFO enthusiasts have been climbing White Sides mountain to a point they term "Freedom Ridge," which rests on public land overlooking Area 51. Believers hope to capture a glimpse of the alien visitors. These people are apparently onto something that the conspiracy does not take well to. On October 6, 1993 the Air Force filed a petition with the Reno, Nevada office of the Bureau of Land Management to withdraw 3,972 acres from public access. The purpose given for the withdrawal was to "ensure the public safety and the safe and secure operation of activities in the Nellis Range Complex." The acreage was White Sides mountain.

Nevada Representative Jim Bilbray was in favor of restricting access to Freedom Ridge. Bilbray, who served on the House Armed Services Committee, said, "Every time someone goes up on White Sides it costs taxpayers a lot of money. They have to cover up what they're doing... with camouflage netting or roll it into the hangars. They have to wait until the people get off the mountain before they can go on with what they're doing."

Shortly after the filing of the petition, Freedom Ridge was closed to the public. The last place that Area 51 can be viewed from is called Tikaboo Peak. Although it is a considerable hike, more and more Dreamland pilgrims undertake the journey every year. Some journey to see flying saucers, others to check the pulse of the conspiracy.

Sources:

"Appeal Expected on Groom Lake," *Las Vegas Review-Journal*, August 28, 1996

Hill Grab, [Online] Available: http:\\www.area51.upsu.plym.ac.uk/~moosie/ufo/txt/lake/040.html

Jacobs, Margaret A., "Desert Battle:A Secret Air Base Hazardous Waste Act, Workers' Suit Alleges," *Wall Street Journal*, February 8, 1996

Knapp, George, "Hangar 18," radio broadcast transcript from KLAS, February 5, 1996

"Memorandum for the Administrator of the Environmental Protection Agency, The Secretary of the Air Force," Presidential Determination No. 95-45, September 29, 1995

Mystery Aircraft, [Online] Available: http:\\www.aemann.demon.co.uk/mysteryaircraft.html

Powers, Francis Gary, *Operation Overflight*

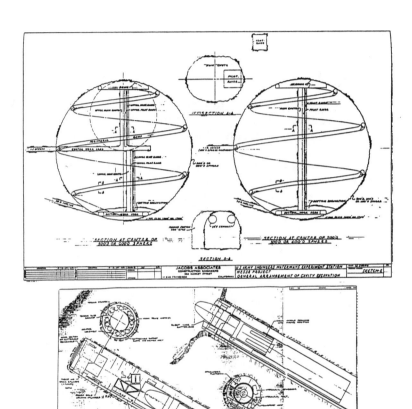

Above: Two methods of constucting a large, deep-underground cavity. Both utilize central shafts, a spiralling perimeter tunnel and work areas at the top and bottom of thea rea to be excavated. Excavation would proceed downward, starting at the top of the designated sphere. From the U.S. Army Corps of Engineers technical manual *Feasibility of Constructing Large Underground Cavities, Vol. III.* Below: An illustration from the U.S. Army Corps of Engineers technical manual *Tunnel Boring Machine Technology for a Deeply Based Missile System. Vol. I, Part 1.* Thanks to Richard Sauder and his book *Underground Bases and Tunnels: What Is the Government Trying To Hide?*

106

(NOTE: This Tesla bulb---a solid aluminum hemisphere excited by high voltage D.C. current---is the basis for the "DEATH RAY" beam, tuned to the T cells of human victims, developed by testing on cows and other livestock... ala "cattle mutilations"... for many years.)

H.V. + or –

I.P.B. (Incident Particle Beam) AXIS

(reversible)

Magnet Field Axis

Electric Field Axis

©WB 1993

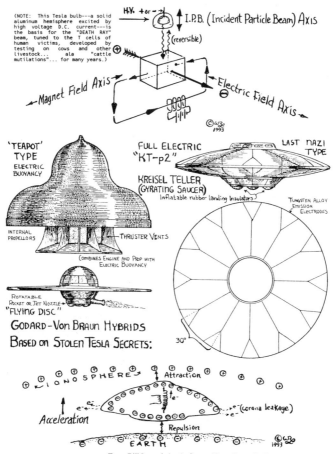

'TEAPOT' TYPE
ELECTRIC BUOYANCY

INTERNAL PROPELLORS

THRUSTER VENTS

COMBINES ENGINE AND PROP WITH ELECTRIC BUOYANCY

ROTATABLE ROCKET OR JET NOZZLE

"FLYING DISC"

GODARD–VON BRAUN HYBRIDS BASED ON STOLEN TESLA SECRETS:

FULL ELECTRIC "KT–p2"

KREISEL TELLER (GYRATING SAUCER)
Inflatable rubber landing insulators

LAST NAZI TYPE

TUNGSTEN ALLOY EMISSION ELECTRODES

30°

IONOSPHERE
Attraction
Acceleration
e⁻ (corona leakage)
Repulsion
EARTH
©WB 1993

From Bill Lynes's book, *Space Aliens From the Pentagon.*

107

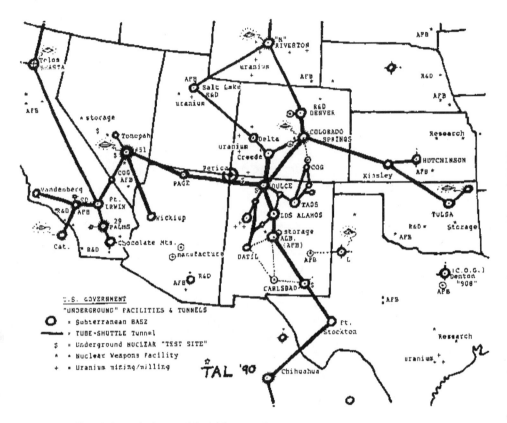

U.S. GOVERNMENT
"UNDERGROUND" FACILITIES & TUNNELS
○ = Subterranean BASE
━ = TUBE-SHUTTLE Tunnel
$ = Underground NUCLEAR "TEST SITE"
∧ = Nuclear Weapons Facility
+ = Uranium mining/milling

TAL '90

Top: A theoretical map of the underground tunnel system in the United States, taken off the Internet. Below: An artist's drawing of a Stealth Fighter with the German insignia on it, also taken from the Internet.

108

CHAPTER NINE

DULCE:
THE HOLE IN THE EARTH

"Troops went in and out of there every summer, starting in '47. The natives do recall that. They also built a road—right in front of the people of Dulce and trucks went in and out for a long period. That Road was later blocked and destroyed.. The signs on the trucks were 'Smith' Corp. out of Paragosa Springs, Colorado. No such corporation exists now—no record exists... I believe the Base—at least the first one was being built then under the cover of a lumbering project... problem—they NEVER hauled logs. Only BIG equipment."

—Paul Bennewitz

There is a massive secret base which is entirely underground near the city of Dulce, New Mexico. Predating Area 51, Dulce is said to be the first alien/human base built in North America. Dulce, from the information that we possess, seems to be primarily a genetic experimentation center which extends 2.5 miles deep into the earth. According to many researchers, aliens exchange technology for animals and humans. And as is the case with Area 51, there are many accounts of alien contact stemming from Dulce.

The story of Philip Schneider is most notable. Schneider was the son of U.S. Navy Captain Oscar Schneider, who had fought on both sides of WW II. As German U-Boat commander, Oscar Schneider was captured and repatriated into the United States Navy where he worked on Nuclear Testing programs in the Bikini Islands, and also was involved in the infamous Philadelphia Experiment.

Philip claims that in 1954 the Eisenhower administration entered into a treaty with an alien race. According to Schneider, the

Grenada Treaty allowed the aliens to use a limited number of humans for experimentation. But the aliens began violating the treaty, and hostilities resulted. These tensions eventually led to a firefight at the Dulce base in 1979.

Schneider says that he worked at the base as a Structural Engineer. While working on an addition to the underground base, he says he stumbled upon a large cavern full of alien humanoids. The aliens were surprised and a battle ensued. There were 66 earthling casualties. Schneider claims to have shot two of the aliens himself, and survived the exchange though he was seriously wounded.

Schneider, according to what he has said, apparently led an extraordinary life. Following his job at Dulce, he found employment at Area 51 where he witnessed the military working with a number of alien spacecraft.

In January of 1996, after two years on the lecture circuit, Schneider was found dead in his Oregon apartment. The official cause of death listed was stroke, but his ex-wife, Cynthia Drayer, believes otherwise:

> I received a call from the Clackamas County Detectives, that the funeral director had found "something" around Philip's neck. An autopsy was performed at the Multnomah County Medical Examiner's office (in Portland, Oregon) by Dr. Gunson, and she determined that Philip had committed suicide by wrapping a rubber catheter hose three times around his neck, and half-knotting it in front. There are several reasons why I believe that Philip did not commit suicide, but was murdered.

Even more outrageous is the data collected by Jason Bishop III. He believes the area is particularly attractive to the aliens because of its location near the Continental Divide, where there is a high concentration of lightning activity, atmospheric ion fields, underground waterways, and cavern systems. The aliens also need the high energy plasma and strong substrata magnetic fields.

"We are leaving the Era of expendable resources, like Oil based products. The Power of the Future is Renewable resources ... 'Biologically' Engineered," says Bishop. "The Dulce Genetic Research was originally funded under the cloak of 'BLACK BUDGET' Secrecy."

Bishop tells that the conspiracy was interested in "intelligent, disposable biology" to perform dangerous atomic and flying saucer experiments. So, using alien technology, the secret government cloned humanoid life forms.

The conspiracy may have staged alien abductions where women were impregnated. The "hybrid fetuses" were removed after three months and their growth was accelerated in the lab. The hybrid humanoids are fitted with brain implants which allow for their control at a distance.

Bishop says that this process was perfected at Los Alamos, which is linked by a "tube-train" to Dulce.

Former Naval Intelligence member William Cooper states that the emblem worn by Dulce security is the Greek letter "Tau" framed inside of a black triangle on a red background. The same insignia has been seen on saucer transport crafts.

Various accounts of the Dulce base describe a multi-leveled hell of bizarre experimentation. There are thousands of humans and human mixtures in cold storage. There are hybrids of humans and animals, genetic nightmares. One worker is quoted as saying: "I have seen multi-legged 'humans' that look like half-human/half-octopus. Also Reptilian-humans, and furry creatures that have hands like humans and cries like a baby, it mimics human words ... also a huge mixture of Lizard-humans in cages."

This description is not unlike the previously mentioned account of MKULTRA victim Lynne Moss-Sharman, giving one pause to think about the possibility of a cross-over between MKULTRA and more unearthly experimentation.

Bishop roomed with Thomas E. Castello—a worker at the Dulce base. Bishop learned from his friend that there are at least 18,000 aliens presently living at the base, working hand-in-hand with the human secret government, and information is highly restricted.

He claims that he met one of the Dulce aliens, a Reptoid, which visited him at his Santa Fe, New Mexico home.

According to Bishop, the Reptoids do not consider themselves extraterrestrial. They consider themselves to be returning to their native home, which is beneath the Earth's surface.

There is a curious tradition of reptile worship amongst secret societies, like the Mesopotamian *Brotherhood of the Snake* which was infiltrated by the original Illuminati thousands of years ago, and the Celtic *Brotherhood of the Serpent*. Reptile intelligence is a theme found in the Old Testament, Egyptian mythology, and Aztec lore.

111

We have discussed Adolph Hitler's fascination with the inner earth. His beliefs regarding the subterranean realm and its black sun are similar to information that exists about the Reptoids. If the Reptoids are inner-terrestrial, that is to say that they are inner-earth beings, then they may have been driven into the earth by the catastrophic occurrence which exterminated their cousins—the dinosaurs. This of course is only speculation.

A possible ancestor of the Reptoids, Leaellynasaura, was discovered by Paleontologist Tom Rich of the Museum of Victoria, Australia. Leaellynasaura was discovered as a 106 million year old fossil found in an excavated tunnel in the south tip of Victoria. The region, 106 million years ago, was part of a southern polar land mass known as Gondwanaland.

This dinosaur had a remarkable ability to adapt to extremes of light and temperature. The creature was unique in a number of ways. It was a bipedal herbivore with long legs and well-developed hands at the end of its front limbs. The creature also had large eyes set into its head.

When Tom Rich discovered Leaellynasaura's skull, he noticed that it also had an unusually large brain for a dinosaur. Nearly 65 percent of the animal's brain was completely dedicated to the processing of optical information, which proved that it could thrive in the long periods of darkness to which the polar region is subject.

If the holes in the poles exist, as Hitler and the Thule theorized, it would have been quite feasible that this creature, along with many others, entered the underworld and continued the evolutionary process, separate from the process occurring above ground. If this is in fact what happened, it may be that this evolution would result in an intelligent, sentient species. One much like the human race, but more ancient.

On March 24, 1990 Nippon Television in Japan aired a two-hour documentary on the Dulce base. A Japanese television crew attempted to find the alleged biogenetics laboratory where they believed existed highly intelligent and deceptive "ultra dimensional entities" which materialized in disguise as aliens. Nippon TV issued that these entities were in collaboration with a secret world government that is preparing to ingeniously stage a contact-landing which will bring about a New World Order.

Though the feature included some slick recreations of what the writers of the show believed existed below ground, the television crew was unable to find the hidden base.

112

Norio Hayakawa was with the television crew during the course of the filming of the special. He had these remarks regarding his experience:

> I've been to Dulce with the Nippon Television Network crew and interviewed many, many people over there and came back with the firm conviction that something was happening around 10 to 15 years ago over there, including nightly sightings of strange lights and appearances of military jeeps and trucks. And I am convinced that the four corners area is a highly occult area. The only stretch of highway, namely Highway 666, runs through the four corners area from southeast Arizona to northwestern New Mexico and up [and into southwest Colorado and southeast Utah]. I have also heard that this Highway 666 came into existence around 1947 or 1948, fairly close to the time of 1947, the modern-day beginning of OVERT UFO APPEARANCE, i.e., the Kenneth Arnold incident.

Hayakawa has interviewed witnesses to the strange activity near Dulce. Military trucks and jeeps are common sights. Some have seen 'CIA types' in black limousines loitering around nearby mesas.

The material on Dulce may be difficult to swallow. Although at moments it seems to fit nicely into the conspiracy puzzle, we have to wonder what the aim of the information might be. Is there a nightmarish lab conducting horrific experiments in Dulce? Does the Dulce base even exist? Or might Dulce be an ostentatious diversion, a sleight of the *unseen hand intended to actually draw us away from the truth of what is going on*?

Evidently, the LC's cover-up of UFOs is becoming increasingly difficult to maintain as more people are involved in it. Some decades ago the conspiracy began applying the technique of *disinformation* to cloud the reality of what was occurring. So that aside from official government denials, there are alternatively a multitude of explanations which are designed to stupefy and malign those who investigate the phenomenon.

For if Dulce does not contain the dreaded alien biogenetics lab we are told of, at the very least it serves as key disinformation.

The truth lies in limbo. Dulce does exist, at least in the minds of the witness accounts. They have seen something terrible: whether this experience occurred in our shared reality or in some crossover twilight world is unknowable at this time. They may be part of a vast web of disinformation, or they may have witnessed hell on earth. Either way, the implications are equally menacing.

Sources:

Cooper, William, *Behold A Pale Horse*
Hayakawa, Norio, "Too Hot Television," Nippon Television Broadcast, March 24, 1990
Reptoids, [Online] Available: http:\\www.reptoids.com
Schneider, Phil, "Aliens & New World Order Conspiracy," a lecture given May 1995
Vardon,Kenneth, "Phillip Schneider Investigation," *Esoteric World News* 1998

The "wink" photograph. Congressman Albert Thomas, responsible for funding NASA, gives Lyndon Johnson a wink shortly after the swearing-in cermony on Air Force One following JFK's assassination. This print was taken from a copy negative held by the LBJ Library in Austin, Texas. The original negative is missing. Photo by Cecil Stoughton.

Von Braun stands with his Mercedes automobile in front of Building 4488 at Redstone Arsenal, Alabama, in 1961. There, both the Army Ballistic Missile Agency and the new NASA-George C. Marshall Space Flight Center shared quarters while the latter's facility was under construction about a mile away. DISC was commanded by von Braun from this building.

115

Chicago Tribune

THE WORLD'S GREATEST NEWSPAPER

The American Paper for Americans

116th YEAR—No. 327 ©© 1963 Chicago Tribune   SATURDAY, NOVEMBER 23, 1963   5   4 SECTIONS—TEN CENTS

ASSASSIN KILLS KENNEDY
LYNDON JOHNSON SWORN IN

35th President

GOVERNOR OF TEXAS WOUNDED; MARXIST ACCUSED OF MURDER

President Shot in Head; Wife by His Side

Sniper Fires 3 Times from 6th Floor Window

BY ROBERT YOUNG
[From Chicago Tribune Press Service]

Dallas, Nov. 22 — President John F. Kennedy was assassinated today.

He was killed by a sniper who ambushed the automobile in which the chief executive and Mrs. Kennedy were riding in a motorcade thru the streets of Dallas. Mrs. Kennedy was unharmed.

Gov. John B. Connally of Texas, riding with the President, was seriously wounded by two shots fired after the bullet which killed the President.

Sworn In on Plane

Kennedy, 46, died at 1 p. m. Chicago time in the emergency

BY WAYNE THOMIS
[From Chicago Tribune Press Service]

Dallas, Nov. 23 [Saturday]—Lee Harvey Oswald, 24, a professed Marxist and Castro follower, was charged late last night with the murder of President Kennedy.

Police Chief Jesse Curry and Homicide Capt. Will Fritz of the Dallas police department made the formal accusation before Justice of the Peace Daniel Johnston. Oswald was held to the grand jury without bail and evidence against him will be presented within the next two or three days.

The action was taken a few minutes before midnight and less than 12 hours after the

36th President

116

CHAPTER TEN

THE DEALY PLAZA BONEYARD

"Apparently something is wrong here!
Something is terribly wrong!"
—Ron Jenkins, reporter for KBOX radio,
first broadcast from the scene of the assassination

There has perhaps been no American leader of this modern age so revered as President John F. Kennedy. As a nation under his leadership we faced both our most triumphant and our most frightening moments. The questions of Kennedy's motivations and morality set aside, his important presence cannot be denied. His term of office was tragically cut short on November 19, 1963. Everyone who was alive on that day remembers where they were when they heard the news, "The President has been shot."

It is for a number of reasons that the people of the world feel cheated by the assassination of JFK. There have been millions of pages written about his murder. A poll conducted in November of 1998 and reported on ABC News demonstrated that 73% of Americans believed that there was a conspiracy involved in Kennedy's assassination. The final stage of grieving is acceptance, and it is due to a number of inconsistencies that we have not been able to accept the death of JFK.

The sometimes ostentatious and disregarding nature the Liquid Conspiracy takes should be heeded. Unlike so many of the LC's victims, Kennedy didn't die of a sudden heart attack. He wasn't killed in an air disaster. His death wasn't attributed to mysterious causes. They killed our President while the whole world was watching.

For those of you unfamiliar with the assassination, if it is possible that anyone could be, I will summarize very briefly the events as reported by the Warren Commission. On November 19, 1963 President John F. Kennedy was riding in an open motorcade with his wife Jacqueline, and Texas Governor John Connally. They were traveling through Dealy Plaza in Dallas when the President and the Governor were both shot. The shots came from a rifle being fired from the southeast sixth floor window of the Texas School Book Depository. The man who fired those shots was said to be the now notorious Lee Harvey Oswald, a self-proclaimed Marxist.

Lee Harvey had brought his weapon to the depository earlier that morning, concealed in a brown paper bag. President Kennedy was first hit by a bullet which entered at the rear of his neck and it exited through the lower front portion of his throat. The second shot that hit JFK struck his head in the lower right area, and caused a massive fatal injury.

Governor Connally was hit by a bullet which entered on the right side of his back and then traveled downward and exited below his right nipple. The bullet then passed through his right wrist and into his left thigh. This bullet may well have been the same bullet that first struck Kennedy.

John F. Kennedy was rushed to a nearby hospital where he was pronounced dead. Governor Connally did survive his injuries and later testified before the Warren Commission.

Forty-five minutes after the Kennedy shooting, Lee Harvey Oswald shot and killed Dallas Police Patrolman J.D. Tippit. Thirty-five minutes later he tried to kill another officer while resisting arrest at a theater.

We will never know Oswald's side of this story. He was snuffed out before he even had a chance to meet with an attorney. At the Dallas Police Department, at 11:21 am on the morning of November 24, Oswald was shot and killed by nightclub owner Jack Ruby.

These are the actual relevant events regarding the assassination of the President, according to the Warren Commission. The commission found no evidence to support any allegations other than the lone gunman scenario. The commission further found that Ruby acted alone and of his own volition when he killed the said assassin. The Warren Commission found that there was no evidence of a conspiracy—of course!

Tippit and Oswald were but the first of many lives claimed by the assassination conspiracy. There exists a collection of mysterious deaths and murders surrounding the assassination and its subsequent investigations. In the three years following the assassination, 18 material witnesses died: six by gunfire, three in motor accidents, two by suicide, one from a cut throat, one from a karate chop, three from heart attacks, and two from natural causes. The *London Sunday Times* reported that the odds of this many witnesses dying were "a trillion to one." Author Jim Marrs, in his book *Crossfire,* documents some 103 deaths connected to the Kennedy assassination, all of which are "strange, mysterious" or "convenient."

In May of 1964 CIA agent Gary Underhill was killed by a gunshot to the head, ruled a suicide. He had made the claim that the CIA was involved in the assassination.

Mona B. Saenz was a Texas Employment clerk who had interviewed Oswald. In August of 1965 she was hit by a bus in Dallas.

Less than three years after the investigation, Lee Bowers, Jr. was killed in an automobile accident. Bowers witnessed the men behind the picket fence on the now famous Grassy Knoll.

Harold Russell died of heart complications following a brawl in a bar involving a policemen. He witnessed the escape of the man who killed Patrolman Tippit.

In the late 1960s, New Orleans District Attorney Jim Garrison brought a case against Clay Shaw, the former OSS operative involved with Operation Paperclip. Garrison accused him of plotting to kill the President. In the end, Garrison's case collapsed; however, according to Marrs, a number of witnesses and officials involved in *that* case have died under suspicious circumstances.

Jim Koethe, a reporter who was in Ruby's apartment on the day Ruby killed Oswald, was killed in September of 1964 by a karate chop to the neck.

Marr's reports that Ruby, who died of cancer, himself relayed to his family that he had been *injected* with lung cancer. Ruby had also been making persistent complaints that he knew of a conspiracy in the death of Kennedy, but that he was not being allowed to tell what he knew. A number of Ruby's employees found themselves on the list as well, including three exotic dancers.

The story of one of these dancers, Rose Cheramie (born Melba Christine Youngblood) warrants retelling. . .

Cheramie was picked up on the evening of November 20, 1963 by Lt. Francis Fruge of the Louisiana State Police. She had been abandoned on highway 190 near Eunice. It was apparent that she had been injured, and though her injuries did not seem life threatening, Fruge thought it prudent to take Cheramie to the Moosa Hospital in Eunice.

Cheramie told the officer that she was en route from Miami to Houston via Dallas when she had an altercation with the two "Latin" men she was riding with. The altercation resulted in her being left on the side of the highway where she was later struck by another car. Her hospital examination found minor abrasions consistent with being struck by an automobile.

Moosa was a private hospital and deemed that the woman had no "financial basis." They informed her that she would be released, not necessarily because she was poor but likely because it had become obvious that she was a drug-addict. She had begun to display symptoms of withdrawal.

For reasons that are unclear, the Assistant Coroner of St. Landry Parish, Dr. F. J. DeRouen was summoned to administer Cheramie a sedative. DeRouen later testified that she had been calm when he was summoned, inconsistent with the prescription. Later that evening DeRouen was again summoned when Cheramie had become violent, stripping off her clothing and cutting her ankles. The Coroner agreed to commit her to the Jackson East Louisiana State Hospital for treatment. Fruge was to accompany her on the one- to two-hour journey.

Officer Fruge asked her a few routine questions. Fruge later testified before the House Select Committee on Assassinations regarding the trip with Cheramie:

> She related to me that she was coming to Dallas with two men who were Italians, or resembled Italians. They had stopped at this lounge and they'd had a few drinks and had gotten into an argument or something. The manger of the lounge threw her out and she got on the road and hitch-hiked to catch a ride, this is when she got hit by a vehicle.

The lounge from which she had been ejected was in fact a brothel called the Silver Slipper. When questioned about her business in Dallas, she replied that she intended to "number one, pick up some

120

money, pick up her baby, and kill Kennedy."

After the assassination Cheramie was taken a bit more seriously. Fruge ordered her not be released from the hospital and interviewed her again. She told the officer that she was working for Jack Ruby, and among other things her work involved running drugs. The two companions she was with were to kill the President and then she was to collect $8,000 from a person whom she refused to identify. The party would then travel to Houston to purchase eight kilos of heroin from a seaman at the port of Galveston. The group planned finally to escape to Mexico.

Rose Cheramie furnished the authorities with the names of her two "Italian" companions, the name of the ship bringing the drugs in, the name of the hotel where the transaction was to take place, and the name of the man who was holding her child. With Cheramie in his custody, Fruge followed up on the information he had been supplied.

Customs officials verified the ship named was in fact due in port, and the identity of the seaman aboard the vessel was confirmed. Customs trailed the sailor but lost track of him. Fruge testified years later that he believed that Customs also verified the name of the man who was allegedly holding Cheramie's son.

While in Fruge's custody Cheramie noticed a headline in a newspaper which indicated that the police had failed to find a connection between Oswald and his killer, Jack Ruby—or "Pinky" as she called him. She told Fruge that she had worked for Ruby, and that he and Oswald had been "shacking up for years ... they were bed-mates."

Fruge reported his findings to Captain Fritz of the Dallas Police Department. Fritz, reasoning that the President's killer had been killed, was not interested.

Rose Cheramie wasn't the only one who had foresight of the assassination. Joseph Milteer, a wealthy right-wing extremist leader in Miami, was also on record with foreknowledge. During taped conversations with a Miami Police Informant named William Somersett on November 9, 1963 Milteer indicated foreknowledge of the planned killing. While the FBI paid no attention to Cheramie's revelations, they were particularly interested in what Milteer had to say. Here are excerpts from the taped discussion. Judge for yourself:

Somersett: ... I think Kennedy is coming here on the 18th ... to make some kind of speech. ...I imagine it will be on

TV.

Milteer: You can bet your bottom dollar he is going to have a lot to say about the Cubans. There are so many of them here.

Somersett: Yeah, well, he will have a thousand bodyguards. Don't worry about that.

Milteer: The more bodyguards he has the more easier it is to get him.

Somersett: Well, how in the hell do you figure would be the best way to get him?

Milteer: From an office building with a high-powered rifle. How many people does he have going around who look just like him? Do you now about that?

Somersett: No, I never heard he had anybody.

Milteer: He has about fifteen. Whenever he goes anyplace, he knows he is a marked man.

Somersett: You think he knows he is a marked man?

Milteer: Sure he does.

Somersett: They are really going to try to kill him?

Milteer: Oh yeah, it is in the working. Brown himself, [Jack] Brown is just as likely to get him as anybody in the world. He hasn't said so, but he tried to get Martin Luther King.

After a few more minutes of conversation, Somersett again spoke of assassination.

Somersett: Hitting this Kennedy is going to be a hard proposition, I tell you. I believe you may have figured out a way to get him, the office building and all that. I don't know how the Secret Service agents cover all them office buildings everywhere he is going. Do you know whether they do that or not?

Milteer: Well, if they have any suspicion they do that, of course. But without suspicion, chances are that they wouldn't. You take there in Washington. This is the wrong time of the year, but in pleasant weather, he comes out of the veranda and somebody could be in a hotel room across the way and pick him off just like that.

Somersett: Is that right?

Milteer: Sure, disassemble a gun. You don't have to take a gun up there, you can take it up in pieces. All those guns come knock down. You can take them apart.

Before the end of the tape, the conversation returns to Kennedy.

Milteer: Well, we are going to have to get nasty ...
Somersett: Yeah, get nasty.
Milteer: We have got to be ready, we have got to be sitting on go, too.
Somersett: Yeah, that is right.
Milteer: There ain't any countdown to it, we have just go to be sitting on go. Countdown, they can move in on you, and on go they can't. Countdown is all right for a slow prepared operation. But in an emergency operation, you have got to be sitting on go.
Somersett: Boy if that Kennedy gets shot, we have got to know where we are at. Because you know that will be a real shake.
Milteer: They wouldn't leave any stone unturned there. No way. They will pick somebody within hours afterwards, if anything like that would happen, just to throw the public off.
Somersett: Oh, somebody is going to have to go to jail, if he gets killed.
Milteer: Just like Bruno Hauptmann in the Lindbergh case, you know.

After JFK's murder Joseph Milteer told the police informant, "Everything ran true to form. I guess you thought I was kidding you when I said he would be killed from a window with a high-powered rifle." When the informant asked him if he was guessing when he originally discussed the topic Milteer replied, "I don't do any guessing."

It is more than curious that Milteer was in Miami making these predictions. If you'll recall, Rose Cheramie was on her way from Miami to Dallas. Might something have been afoot in the Miami underground?

It also interesting to note, if not purely for entertainment, that Cheramie refers to Jack Ruby as "Pinky" and the named assassin in Milteer's conversation is "Jack Brown." Colorful ...

Time and convenient deaths have allowed for so much cover-up and disinformation which prevents the incrimination of those responsible parties for the assassination of President Kennedy, and I cannot in good conscience lend what is simply an opinion about the true identity of those guilty. Many researchers have devoted their life's work to the question and I would be doing them a disservice by writing what boils down to speculation. Just about everyone under the sun has been accused of pulling the trigger: the mob, the CIA, the FBI, the Soviets, etc. I can only recommend that you, the reader, familiarize yourself with some of the many scenarios, as they will at least prove that there is indeed a dark, secretive and deadly power lurking just behind the curtains.

Sources:

Baton Rouge Morning Advocate ... [Online] Available:
    http:\\www.mcadams.posc.mu.edu/russo1.txt
Crossfire: Convenient Deaths [Online] Available:
    http:\\www.informatik.uni-rostock.de/Kennedy/deaths.html
JFK assassination research files [Online] Available:
    http:\\www.home.earthlink.net/~clintbrad4d/
Marrs, Jim, Crossfire
Mills, Chris, Rambling Rose
Milteer txt [Online] Available:
    http:\\www.mcadams.posc.mu.edu/milteer.txt

Cord Meyer.

Mary Pinchot Meyer.

Mary Pinchot Meyer with Cord Meyer.

Mary Pinchot Meyer with John F. Kennedy.

CHAPTER ELEVEN

SEX, DRUGS, AND UFOS

Just who shot JFK may never be known, although there was certainly no lack of motives for the killing. Though the motives can hardly be used to identify the perpetrator or perpetrators, they do shed light and permit focus on some conspicuous activities that the LC would rather you not notice.

Particularly of interest to popular culture is the alleged affair between President Kennedy and Hollywood starlet Marilyn Monroe. Details of the relationship expose one of the more bizarre episodes in modern history.

On May 19, 1962, the President publicly celebrated his birthday at Madison Square Garden. There were 15,000 people in attendance and no doubt that there were at least a few eyebrows raised when Marilyn Monroe sang her steamy version of *Happy Birthday*. She was dressed in a $5,000 flesh colored dress which she was literally sewn into. At the conclusion of this serenade, Mr. President was moved to say "Thank you. I can now retire from politics after having had Happy Birthday sung to me in such a sweet, wholesome way."

John F. Kennedy's love affair with Marilyn Monroe may have begun as early as 1955. There were numerous rendezvous at the President's New York City apartment in the Carlyle Hotel. The couple also stayed together at the home of Peter Lawford. Though it is said that Monroe would find a deeper love in her affair with Jack's brother, the Attorney General Robert Kennedy, her fling with the President is now one of history's most notorious moments.

Marilyn Monroe kept details of the time that she shared with the Kennedys.

While their relationship may be sensational, there existed concern for the public consequence. The ramifications of JFK's private excursions with Marilyn Monroe have been explored in two recent

Kennedy biographies, one written by Thomas Reeves, a professor at the University of Wisconsin, and one by Seymour Hersh, a former investigative reporter for the *New York Times* and a Pulitzer Prize winner.

Both writers conclude that Kennedy's indiscriminate liaisons endangered national security by subjecting him to possible blackmail. Furthermore, the authors suggest that Kennedy distanced himself from national security officials, who may have been required at a moment's notice to assist with an emergency, because he was forced to hide information about his trysts. Might there have been a national security issue warranting the death of Marilyn Monroe?

In his 1991 book *A Question of Character*, Reeves writes:

> Kennedy's personal foibles... were dangerous to the welfare of this country and the free world. While we know of only one specific case in which the president was separated from the official who carries the secret information vital to the nation's nuclear defense, and is supposed to be near the chief executive at all times, such incidents surely happened often in the course of Jack's clandestine prowlings. When the president ... was roaming through the tunnels beneath New York's Carlyle Hotel to evade reporters and reach intimate friends, was he prepared to handle national security matters?

In *The Dark Side of Camelot*, Hersh conveys that the President's roving eye made it possible for hostile intelligence forces to gather information from the highest source possible. Might that exact situation have in fact occurred? Almost with certainty it happened at least once.

Aside from Marilyn, President Kennedy had a number of alleged flings. One such affair was supposed to be with Ellen Rometsch, an East German who bore a striking resemblance to actress Elizabeth Taylor. Rometsch was attending late night pool parties at the White House when the FBI suspected her of being a communist spy. Rometsch was abruptly deported on August 21, 1963.

So was Marilyn Monroe a national security threat? A consensus of researcher's opinions will confirm this possibility. Monroe was reportedly connected to the mobster Sam Giancana through another lover of hers, Frank Sinatra. The underworld figure frequently stayed at Sinatra's Lake Tahoe Casino/Hotel the *Cal Neva*. (Monroe completed her last film, *The Misfits*, in Reno, Nevada, less than an hour's drive from Lake Tahoe.)

Attorney General Robert Kennedy had begun a serious legal campaign against organized crime, naming Giancana suspect. The name appears often in JFK assassination theories, due, in part, to Giancana's ties to the CIA. The CIA had contracted the mobster in a failed plot to "hit" Fidel Castro. Giancana also had a business relationship with Lee Oswald's assailant, Jack Ruby. Kennedy's presidential campaign was in part financed by Giancana, to the tune of millions of dollars. There can be no doubt that extreme tensions ensued when Robert Kennedy initiated his prosecution. But might the Giancana connection be a scapegoat for something much more bizarre? There exists a government document suggesting just that.

In 1962, the FBI had been monitoring the telephone conversations of Monroe, Robert Kennedy, and the Hollywood columnist Dorothy Kilgallen. During a conversation with Howard Rothberg, Kilgallen discussed a number of items which kept the report Top Secret for many years. Aside from reporting the "break up with the Kennedys" the document tells of Marilyn Monroe's visit to a "secret airbase" where Kennedy took her to inspect "things from outer space."

FBI director J. Edgar Hoover made no secret of his contempt for Robert Kennedy. He had agents wiretap all of his telephone calls. Wiretap recordings of RFK's conversations with Monroe confirm the document's validity.

The top-secret report mentions that Monroe threatened to hold a press conference to "tell all." This fact is confirmed by a number of witnesses to Monroe's last day on Earth.

The mysterious document is dated August 3, 1962—the day before Marilyn's "suicide." It has been suggested that Monroe was killed for her threat to reveal her secrets to the public. Might the danger of those secrets have had more to do with the "crashed spaceship and dead bodies" than of her obvious affairs with the Kennedy brothers?

Her body was discovered at her home at 12305 Fifth Helena Drive. Her death was ruled a "Probable Suicide." Although her autopsy report described her as a "well nourished Caucasian female, weighing 117 pounds and measuring 65 and half inches in length," she was supposed to have died due to an overdose of the barbiturate Nembutal, and of the drug Chloral Hydrate.

Chloral Hydrate was also used by the mob on at least one recorded occasion. They slipped the drug to a politician in 1961 to discredit him. Where do you suppose the Mafia learned how to control the mind with the use of drugs? There is a significant likeness here to CIA MKULTRA research, and as demonstrated by the previously mentioned "hit" on Castro, the agency had a relevant relationship with the mob.

There are no photographs remaining of Monroe's autopsy. The phone records from her last days are gone. Although there were three empty pill bottles by her bedside, there was no drinking glass discovered at the scene and the plumbing in her bathroom was known to be inoperative. There is no routine death report left behind. The files were taken by Chief Parker to Washington D.C. to "show to somebody." They have never resurfaced.

The determination that Marilyn committed suicide is questionable at best. The coroner Dr. Noguchi said that he felt uncomfortable with the decision. For one, although the levels of the drugs were high in her blood, there was no residue of the capsules in her stomach or intestines. To add to that suspicious circumstance, there were no injection marks either. The only remaining means of ingestion was an enema. In her last days Marilyn often took enemas because of extreme constipation.

The woman lived a very sad life beneath the glamorous surface. Although Marilyn was loved by millions, she had been used like a whore by some of the world's most powerful men. She was fired from movie studios during the last days. She had failed to even show up for filming except for one out of every three days. There are reports indicating that Monroe was taking up to 20 sleeping pills a day to cope. She reportedly believed that Robert Kennedy would eventually leave his wife and family to marry her. The world's most celebrated beauty was strung along like a storybook mistress. She did indeed possess the desperation to end her own life, but there remains a large body of questions surrounding her death which are to this day unanswered.

Might Marilyn Monroe's trip with Jack Kennedy to the "secret airbase" be substantial? Could her remarks be attributed to drug induced delusions for which the Mob or the CIA may have been responsible? Or did JFK really take Marilyn to somewhere like Area 51 to show off his presidential prowess?

In any event, Marilyn Monroe was apparently not alone in her experimentation with drugs. The 35th President of the United States had yet another relationship, from which unthinkable questions have arisen.

130

During project MKULTRA, as the CIA was experimenting with LSD, the agency set up projects through a number of prestigious universities. One such university was Harvard, where Professor Timothy Leary first "tripped out." One of the many people whom Leary introduced to LSD was Mary Pinchot Meyer.

Deborah Davis, author of *Katherine the Great, Katherine Graham and Her Washington Post Empire*, describes Meyer as "a very beautiful, talented artist." She was living in Washington during Kennedy's term as President. Davis asserts that John was very much in love with Mary. She claims that he wanted to divorce Jackie in order to marry Meyer.

Mary Meyer told Leary of her grand scheme to "turn on" major figures in the government. She believed that the drug would make them better, wiser, holier leaders. She had insisted her plan was already set in motion, in fact she stated, "you'd be amazed" about who she had tripped with.

Mary Meyer's ex-husband was Cord Meyer, a high-ranking CIA agent not surprisingly involved in the LSD experimentation phases of MKULTRA. The two were divorced due to an affair she had with an Italian intelligence official while the couple was living in Europe. It was decided that her marriage to Cord was a security risk. (Familiar theme?)

Shortly after John Kennedy was assassinated, Mary was murdered. While walking her dog through a wooded area of Georgetown, she was stabbed to death. Her killer has never been found, and the diaries she kept have disappeared. It seems that information regarding Kennedy's alleged mistresses often disappears.

Researcher Kenn Thomas writes about Mary Meyer and JFK in *King Leary*. He informs us that Mary Pinchot Meyer was JFK's "last lover" and that she "apparently brought him pot and LSD." He quotes Kennedy speaking to Meyer, "This isn't at all like cocaine. I'll get you some of that."

Is it possible that JFK was experimenting with LSD? There seems to be evidence to suggest just that. More than likely though, the CIA was experimenting with the President. When Kennedy was elected President of the United States his influence posed a threat to the power structure of the intelligence community. After the Bay of Pigs fiasco, it has been suggested, there was a growing rift between the two. I would venture to take that one step further and suggest that the Bay of Pigs invasion may have been intentionally botched in order to unify the agency against the President. It is this author's opinion that President Kennedy was a decent and charismatic man who fell victim to the right hand of the LC.

A number of conspiratorial dots should be connected here, linking the CIA to the scene of the President's murder. Clay Shaw was indicted by District Attorney Jim Garrison in New Orleans for the crime of assassinating the President. He himself was a former OSS operative, involved in Operation Paperclip, and had ties to the FBI and the CIA.

Of the three tramps picked up at the Grassy Knoll, all have been named as intelligence connections. One of them, identified during the Warren Commission Hearings, was Fred Crisman. Remember Crisman? He was the man who switched the debris of the Maury Island flying saucer incident before it was passed on to military investigators. What was *he* doing at Dealy Plaza the day Kennedy was shot?

New Orleans District Attorney Jim Garrison wanted to know the answer to that question, as well. According to a 1968 wire report, Garrison subpoenaed Fred Crisman of Tacoma, Washington to testify at Clay Shaw's Grand Jury. Crisman was identified as a radio announcer, but Garrison's investigation implied that he was either a member of the CIA or had been "engaged in undercover activity for a part of the industrial warfare complex." Crisman allegedly operated as a preacher engaged in work to help the Gypsies.

The exact nature of Crisman's involvement with the assassination is not known. He never actually testified in Clay Shaw's trial. The conspiracy made sure of that.

Whose interests did the death of our most beloved leader benefit? Whose interest did concealing the Maury Island UFO debris serve?

And so we come full circle, back to the flying saucer connection. Were John F. Kennedy and Marilyn Monroe killed to protect this century's most guarded secret? They wouldn't have been the first, nor the last. The LC seems determined to guard their secrets, their stolen technology, their unspoken agenda. No one will stand in their path to world domination. They have learned well from the leaders whom they've toppled. There is no phoenix to lift hope from the tragic murder of President Kennedy. Simply, from the ashes of Camelot a stronger, incontestable conspiracy has arisen.

Sources:

Arkansas Connections: A Timeline of the Clinton Years by Sam
    Smith [Online] Available: http:\ \
    www.emporium.turnpike.net/P/ProRev/connex.html
The Assassination of JFK [Online] Available:
    http:\ \www.members.aol.com/maxqc/anglais/assassinat/jfk1.ht
    ml
Biographers Study Presidential Promiscuity [Online] Available:
    http:\ \www.toledoblade.com/editorial/clinton/8a25prom.html
The Final Act (1960-1962) [Online] Available:
    http:\ \www.members.aol.com/monroe1fan/biography/the_fina
    l_act.html
The Fourth Decade [Online] Available:
    http:\ \www.mcadams.posc.mu.edu/sleuth.txt
Happy Birthday Mr. President [Online] Available:
    http:\ \www,members.aol.com/JFKin61/birthday.html
An Interview with Deborah Davis [Online] Available:
    http:\ \www.umsl.edu/~skthoma/hpage.html
Kannon, Gregory M., The candle burns down, the death of Marilyn
    Monroe [Online] Available: http:\ \www.guinness-stout.com/m-
    doc.cfm
Mary Pinchot Meyer: A Rock Opera [Online] Available:
    http:\ \www.concentric.net/~moviebam/mpm.html
Secrets of the Mohave [Online] Available:
    http:\ \www.anomalous-images.com/text/mojave12.html
Thomas, Kenn, *King Leary*
Webber, Conrad, *The Laymen's Blue Book*, Hysteria, Australia, 1987

Senator Robert F. Kennedy lying dead on the floor of the hotel kitchen. The clip-on tie of his body-guard Thane Cesar can be seen near his right hand.

Sirhan Sirhan is taken into custody immediately after the shooting.

David Chapman: John Lennon's mind control killer?

A court drawing of David Chapman.

SPECIAL REPORT UFO'S, COMETS AND CULTS

Newsweek

'Follow Me'

INSIDE THE HEAVEN'S GATE MASS SUICIDE

Heaven's Gate: Mind Control & UFOs.

Jim Jones: A CIA mind control project?

CHAPTER TWELVE

MIND KONTROLLED KILLERS ON THE RAMPAGE

"There was a running interest in what effects people's standing in the field of radio energy have, and it could easily have been that somewhere in the many projects someone was trying to see if you could hypnotize somebody easier if he was standing in a radio beam."
–Dr. Sidney Gottlieb, MKULTRA director, before the Senate Subcommittee on Health and Scientific Research on September 21, 1977

"Do it, Do it, Do it."
—the voice in Mark David Chapman's head immediately before he killed John Lennon

One of the goals of the Central Intelligence Agency's MKULTRA was to develop the ability to program assassins. Given the benefit of the doubt, one would assume these assassins would be used to remove enemy leaders of nations hostile to our own. What if the sole purpose of this research was to develop a mind controlled slave who could kill anyone who stood in the way of the CIA? The potential exists that this slave's mind could be "emptied" after pulling the trigger, leaving a seemingly psychotic individual caught red-handed. Given the evidence of the CIA's pursuit of mind control, and the existing electromagnetic brain implant technology, the feasibility of the Programmed Assassin is apparent.

Furthermore, there is substantial proof that this nation's most famous assassins were themselves victims of mind control. Today one can retrieve copies of any number of patents granted to designers of mind control apparatuses from the U.S. Patent Office. The work of Jose Delgado, John Lilly, and a host of Nazi scientists have proven the potential of such an inquiry. Might men like Lee Harvey Oswald, Sirhan Sirhan, and John Hinckley been at the mercy of exterior control?

In the classic underground conspiracy book *Were We Controlled?*^ author Lincoln Lawrence explores one such scenario. It is the story behind the Kennedy assassination story. According to Lawrence, Lee Harvey Oswald was programmed to kill the President of the United States as part of an experiment of a secret group using a combination of Radio Hypnotic Intercerebral Control and Electronic Dissolution of Memory (RHIC-EDOM).

Lee Harvey Oswald lived a mysterious life leading into 1963. He had served in this country's armed services as a self-proclaimed Marxist. He defected to the Soviet Union with his wife Marina Oswald. He had made trips to Mexico to seek political asylum. Oswald lived under continuous governmental observation, whether here or abroad. For one reason or another, the intelligence community took an interest in Lee Harvey Oswald.

While in jail after being arrested for the murder of Kennedy, Oswald told interrogators of the FBI's harassment of his wife. The records confirm that the FBI did indeed visit the residence where the Oswalds were staying on several occasions. The KGB also kept Oswald under continuous scrutiny, as evidenced by a multitude of surveillance photographs.

So why all of the interest in the man? If you should answer that question by saying that Oswald was a dangerous man and the government wanted to keep him under watch, why then did they let him kill the President?

Lawrence answers the question by stating that Lee Harvey Oswald received a RHIC-EDOM brain implant which manipulated his behavior with suggestions radioed into his mind, and then was capable of erasing his memory of events.

CIA Director McCone wrote a memo to Secret Service director James Rowley in 1964, stating that Oswald had possibly been "chemically or electronically controlled ... a sleeper agent. [Oswald] spent 11 days hospitalized for a minor ailment which should have required no more than three days hospitalization at best." Lawrence indicates that when Lee Harvey was "put under" at the Ear Nose and Throat Hospital in Minsk, Russia, he was implanted with a tiny radio receiver which would trigger previously induced post-hypnotic suggestions.

It is true that Oswald spent an excessive amount of time in a Soviet hospital for what was supposed to be an ear infection. Oswald's brother noted that his hair had changed when he came back from Russia, that it had not only thinned, but the texture had changed.

It would also not be unreasonable to speculate that Lee Harvey Oswald could have been part of the MKULTRA experiments, given the fact that a major emphasis on the work was the creation of mind controlled assassins.

In September of 1957 Oswald arrived at the United States Naval Air Base in Atsugi, Japan, where MKULTRA LSD experiments were said to occur. Atsugi was also the launching place for the U-2 spy plane. Oswald was given a security clearance and worked as a radar operator on the base. This was odd, as Oswald was an outspoken communist, so much so that he was dubbed "Oswaldovitch."

While at a Tokyo nightclub Oswald became intimate with a woman now believed to have been a spy for the Soviet Union. He subsequently contracted gonorrhea. Do you recall the MKULTRA LSD trials of Operation Midnight Climax?

Oswald's assailant, Jack Ruby, may have been a victim of mind control also. In Dealy Plaza just prior to the JFK assassination was the hypnotist William Crowe, who worked under the stage name of Bill DeMar. Crowe was performing at Jack Ruby's Carousel Club the week leading into Kennedy's murder. It has been suggested that Crowe may have programmed Ruby to kill Oswald.

If JFK's death didn't seem fishy enough, consider the murder of his brother Bobby. Robert Kennedy had served as the United States Attorney General. His claim to fame was taking on the mob during Grand Jury hearings on organized crime. In 1968, Senator Robert Kennedy was campaigning for the office of President of the United States. He was apparently gunned down by Sirhan Sirhan, a Palestinian Arab, on June 5th just after midnight.

Robert Kennedy had just won the Californian Democratic Primary and he was about to make a victory speech. While he was making his way through the pantry area of the Ambassador Hotel to a press conference, Sirhan stepped toward the Senator and fired a .22 caliber revolver at him.

Sirhan was arrested on the scene. He was charged and convicted of first degree murder. Sirhan was sentenced to execution, but the

Supreme Court ruled that the death penalty was unconstitutional before the sentence could be carried out. Under California law, Sirhan was scheduled for release in 1984, but this was not to be the case. Sirhan has been denied parole after 10 hearings.

The Sirhan family held a press conference on June 5, 1998, marking the 30th anniversary of the assassination. Most notable in the conference were the remarks made by Sirhan's brother Adel, who said that Sirhan was not the man who shot the Senator that night. "He is an innocent man," Adel says.

Most recently, Sirhan Sirhan's attorney, Larry Teeter, has filed a petition for a Writ of Habeas Corpus in a California Court of Appeals. Teeter argues that a massive cover-up occurred which involved evidence tampering and suppression on behalf of the prosecution.

Teeter goes so far as to suggest that Sirhan was hypnotized by unknown persons to act as a patsy.

Is it possible that like his brother's, Robert Kennedy's death may have to be blamed on a mind controlled puppet?

According to modern psychedelic guru Terrance McKenna, Sirhan Sirhan made his way through the state mental hospital in Vacaville, California where none other than Timothy Leary was conducting drug trials on behalf of the CIA.

In his book *The RFK Assassination,* author Professor Phil Melanson issues:

> It appears that the CIA carried out experiments in the Fifties and also in the Sixties, to test the possibility of hypnotically programming murders. And that it had succeeded during the course of its experiments in determining that people could be hypnotically induced to perform reprehensible acts without having any memory that they committed these acts. If that's the case then it would have been possible for someone to program someone like Sirhan Sirhan or anybody else who is a suitable subject to walk into a pantry, pull out a gun and begin pulling the trigger. From the very beginning there had been powerful suggestions, advanced from a number of quarters, that Sirhan may had been in some sort of trance-like state. When driving to the police station in Sirhan Sirhan's company, Sirhan Sirhan was observed by Jesse Unruh, a powerful Californian politician, who

said that Sirhan Sirhan appeared to be in some sort of a trance. Once in police custody, he was placed under hypnosis later on by defense psychiatrist Dr. Diamond. And he behaved in a way to cause Dr. Diamond to conclude, that Sirhan Sirhan had been hypnotised.

Repeatedly scribbled into Sirhan's personal diary prior to the murder, are the words "RFK must die." What could have motivated Sirhan Sirhan to murder Bobby Kennedy? The official line is that he was upset over the sale of warplanes to Israel that the senator had approved. But this was not a murder well planned and executed. The timing was inopportune, and the execution was sloppy. Sirhan was certainly not a political assassin. He was a man driven to insanity by something which has not been brought to light publicly.

To test this mind control hypothesis, we need to determine the CIA's motivation for eliminating Robert Kennedy. Instead of asking why Sirhan Sirhan killed RFK, we should ask, *Why would the CIA want to assassinate the Presidential hopeful?*

Larry Teeter, one of Sirhan's current attorneys, proposes:

> The people who benefited from this assassination were primarily those who wanted to keep the war in Vietnam going. That would be the CIA and the military, because Robert Kennedy promised that if he was elected president he would stop the war in Vietnam.

So because the CIA had an interest in continuing the war, they sought to pull Robert Kennedy out of the race. How they accomplished this is a matter of speculation. We can simply conclude from the evidence that exists that the CIA has an interest in continuing the cover-up.

Most peculiar is a recent development that stems from a 1997 television program produced by CBS television. Two newsmen—Philip Shimkin, a CBS producer in New York, and Robert Beuchler, of CBS News in San Francisco—had written to Sirhan Sirhan in prison, asking for an interview based on his recent and new claim of innocence at his last parole hearing.

Sirhan passed the letter on to Rose Lynn Mangan, his personal researcher who had a limited power of attorney. Mangan contacted CBS television and asked them to send a letter stating their intentions. The response contained little information, simply stating that they wanted an interview with Sirhan Sirhan to discuss developments in his case for a segment on Bryant Gumbel's show *Public Eye.*

Rose Lynn Mangan responded that prison rules did not generally allow television interviews of prisoners, but that the journalists could come to see Sirhan as visitors. She forwarded the proper requisite forms to them.

The two men went to see Sirhan in the company of Mangan, Sirhan's brother, and attorney Larry Teeter. During the conversation, CBS suggested staging a "chance encounter" with Sirhan where they could happen upon him in the yard, and film through the fence.

Now, a true chance encounter with a prisoner in a public area is not prohibited in the Californian prison. Suspicious, Mangan asked Teeter to follow up with the Department of Corrections. She stated that she would only recommend that Sirhan give an interview if CBS obtained written permission from the prison warden.

Larry Teeter wrote to the Department of Corrections, informing them of the proposed plan (without mentioning CBS or the people involved by name) and asked the Department for guidance.

The response came from a Senior Staff Counsel, saying that while the media "may interview randomly encountered inmates in general population areas, [the Department] vigorously objects to any plans to circumvent the Department's media policy, i.e., by prearranging to have a specific inmate present at a particular place and time."

In response to the question of what the resulting punishment might be for such an event, the Department responded, "Enforcement of these policies include disciplinary action against the inmate and statewide exclusion of the media or legal personnel involved."

If Sirhan Sirhan agreed to go ahead with the staged encounter, he might have been cut off from his lawyer, his family, his researcher, and the media he was hoping to reach.

Lisa Pease, in her *Probe* article, "CBS and the RFK Case" writes:

> Why would CBS propose such a scheme? Was this approach genuinely based in a serious interest in the case, or was some other motivation at work? Shimkin and Buechler had shown particular interest in some of Mangan's latest research, but when she showed it to

them they immediately strove to find fault with it, hardly the kind of objective approach for which the group had been hoping. The CBS men suggested hiring their own expert to examine the findings in Mangan's research. Mangan said that she would want to be present at the examination. This suggestion caused the men to suggest that would be tantamount to having Mangan run the show. As the evidence is extremely complex, Mangan wanted to be present herself to make sure that were there any questions, she would be available to answer and explain, rather than have someone guess and misinterpret what she had presented. When the CBS men flatly refused this offer, Mangan, who for years has felt that nothing would be a greater boon to this case than some serious publicity, balked, and told them "Give me back my papers." The men went into shock, not dreaming she could be serious. They told her that the very papers they had earlier ridiculed were critical to the show's success, and that they would not do a segment if she withdrew the papers at this time. "Give me back my papers," Mangan repeated. She also suggested that CBS hire *three* experts, not just *one*. She suggested as an additional two both Cyril Wecht and Henry Lee, forensic experts whom she felt would do their best to deal honestly with the evidence. Using only one expert left the door open for a rigged situation, or suspicions of such. The men refused to assent to any of these suggestions, and drove off visibly perturbed by what had transpired. The Sirhan brothers, Teeter, and Mangan herself were predictably disappointed. Perhaps they would have been less so had they remembered the broadcast CBS did on the Sirhan case back in 1975.

In 1975, after the Church and Pike committee investigations of the CIA, CBS television produced a series entitled *The American Assassins*, with host Dan Rather. The first part of the series concerned the John F. Kennedy assassination. There was an episode on the Martin Luther King assassination. The final program was about the Robert Kennedy assassination, and the attempt on Governor George Wallace's life in 1972.

CBS dealt with some of the major problems with the JFK and

MLK assassinations, but concerning RFK stated, "One day, at least this case may be stamped completely closed in the minds of most reasonable Americans."

In the underground, the CIA have long been suspected of involvement in the 1960s assassinations. There can be no doubt that the Liquid Conspiracy has aimed to control the media. If one follows the trail from the Sirhan Sirhan coverage from CBS, he will stumble upon an empire ruled by none other than the Central Intelligence Agency.

According to Lisa Pease, the CIA has had a long and close working relationship with CBS.

Further documentation can be found in Carl Bernstein's *Rolling Stone Magazine* article, entitled "The CIA and the Media." He writes:

> CBS was unquestionably the CIA's most valuable broadcasting asset. CBS President William Paley and Allen Dulles enjoyed an easy working and social relationship. Over the years, the network provided cover for CIA employees, including at least one well-known foreign correspondent and several stringers. ...Once a year during the 1950's and early 1960's, CBS correspondents joined the CIA hierarchs for private dinners and briefings.

The Bernstein article said that in 1976 the president of CBS News, Richard Salant, also president during the 1975 documentary, asked for an in-house investigation of his network's ties with the CIA. Astonishingly, Salant's report made no mention of some of his own dealing with the Agency, which drifted into the 1970s. Bernstein continues:

> In 1964 and 1965, Salant served on a supersecret CIA task force which explored methods of beaming American propaganda broadcasts to the People's Republic of China. The other members of the four-man study team were Zbigniew Brzezinski [directly tied to the LC's 1945 Geneva meeting], then a professor at Columbia University; William Griffith, then professor of political science at Massachusetts Institute of Technology; and John Hayes, then vice-president of the Washington Post

Company for radio-TV. The principal government officials associated with the project were Cord Meyer of the CIA; McGeorge Bundy, then special assistant to the president for national security; Leonard Marks, then director of USIA; and Bill Moyers, then special assistant to President Lyndon Johnson and now a CBS correspondent.

What about America's favorite CBS news correspondent? Daniel Schorr wrote about an incident in his book *Clearing the Air:*

> [T]he luncheon that Paley held in his private dining room on the thirty-fifth floor on February 4, 1976, for George Bush, the new CIA director, did not go as he had hoped. What was to be a sociable welcome for the son of the late Senator Prescott Bush, warmly remembered as an early CBS board member, turned, after dessert, into an argument about CIA agents posing as reporters. It was started by Walter Cronkite, angry because he had been identified by a former television newsman, Sam Jaffe, as having appeared on an alleged White House list of journalists who had purportedly worked for the CIA. To remove the stain on him and on journalism, Cronkite demanded that Bush disclose the list of news people who actually had been CIA agents.

Prescott Bush—early CBS board member? His son George Bush—Director of the CIA? The lines between CBS and the intelligence agencies of this country run deep. We can be certain that the tentacles reach into other news camps as well. Don't forget that the Nazi scientist Wernher von Braun, inventor of the V-2 rocket which terrorized the English people in World War II, ended up on television hosting Disney's weekly entertainment program, thanks to the fine people of the CIA and their Operation Paperclip! Remember that every major news service is headed by members of the Council on Foreign Relations, which came into being through Cecil Rhodes's Round Table. Rhodes had direct ties to Tavistock, the home base of 20th century mind control.

Are the two CBS newsmen the "shock troops" that were promised by Major John Rawlings Reese? Are they participating in *society* by continuing the manipulation of public opinion regarding the RFK assassination?

Just as an organism contains a DNA blueprint in every cell, the Liquid Conspiracy's plan is hidden within every deed.

The aim of the Liquid Conspiracy is TOTAL CONTROL. They control the CIA which controlled the mind of Sirhan Sirhan, and the media, which in turn controls your opinions and beliefs.

And what of John Hinckley, Jr.? Was the man who tried to fill President Ronald Reagan with lead a programmed assassin? What prompted this disturbed young man to try to kill the President of the United States? John Hinckley's road has led him to a life sentence in a mental hospital, but did he get there of his own accord?

It is interesting to note that John's father was reportedly a friend of George Bush. It is important to remember that then-Vice President George Bush had previously headed up the Central Intelligence Agency, which in itself may not seem relevant, but when placed alongside the assassin's profile, paints a suspicious picture. George Bush was just a heartbeat away from becoming President before his time.

Curiously, when John Hinckley, Jr. shot the President, he had just been released from a federal mental hospital. Could he have been programmed at this institution like so many others of MKULTRA were?

Reportedly he was photographed with one of the Bush boys at a pro-Nazi rally. What do these family ties mean? Hinckley gives his reason for the assassination attempt as a means to impress Jodi Foster, the actress he was stalking. But is there perhaps a more sinister scenario at work?

There are reports that John Hinckley, Jr. had a "twin" in New York City. According to the account, a man who physically resembled Hinckley was apprehended by police in a New York City subway. He was waving a gun and threatening to kill the President, while John was in Washington D.C. carrying out the same plan. He, like Hinckley, had an obsession for Jodi Foster, and a fixation on the book *Catcher in the Rye*.

Another fan of *Catcher* was Mark David Chapman, the young man who shot and killed former Beatle John Lennon. According to researcher Jim Keith in *Mind Control, World Control*, Chapman may have been a mind controlled assassin.

Lennon was a target of the United States government for some years. He had an extensive FBI file before the CIA began observing him in 1972. The former Beatle had been quite vocal in his opposition

146

to the Vietnam War and was seen as an effective force capable of rallying the American youth.

On February 23, 1972, an agent of the Central Intelligence Agency filed the following report:

> Some American participants at the Soviet-controlled World Assembly for Peace and Independence of the Peoples of Indochina, held 11-13 February 1972 in Paris/Versailles, attempted unsuccessfully to include a call for international demonstrations to take place at the time of the Republican National Convention. ...
>
> John LENNON, a British subject, has provided financial support to Project YES, which in turn paid the travel expenses to the World Assembly of a representative of leading anti-war activists (and Chicago-Seven defendant) Rennie DAVIS. ... In Paris this representative in the World Assembly met at least once with officials of the Provisional Revolutionary Government of South Vietnam; it is not known if the Republican Convention was discussed.

Later that year John Lennon told friend Paul Krassner, "Listen, if anything happens to Yoko and me, it was not an accident." Clearly, Lennon was concerned for his life. The United States sought Lennon's deportation to Britain because of a supposed marijuana violation. Lennon made it known that he believed the true intention of the United States was to squelch his anti-war voice, and fought being deported vehemently.

In a memo now public, with the exception of large, suspiciously marked-out segments, FBI supervisor E.L. Shackleford wrote:

> In view of the successful delaying tactics to date, there exists real possibility that subject [Lennon] will not be deported from U.S. in near future and possibly not prior to Republican National Convention. Subject's activities being closely followed and any information developed indicating violation of Federal laws will be immediately furnished to pertinent agencies in effort to neutralize any disruptive activities of subject.

In 1973 the United States Department of Justice admitted that John Lennon's telephone was illegally wiretapped.

John Lennon, in an effort to preserve his family, reluctantly pulled out of political activism and essentially went into a life of seclusion until 1980. The fires rekindled within Lennon however, and with the release of his latest album he had become active again.

Lennon's harassment from the U.S. government cannot be understated. One can imagine that the assassination plot is outlined underneath the blacked-out paragraphs among the thousands of paragraphs in top-secret documents the U.S. government has written. Might he have been slated for elimination, in the name of national security?

John Lennon's killer, Mark David Chapman, was a world traveler. He was a born-again Christian employed by the YMCA in the 1970s. He worked as a humanitarian in different missions around the globe. After a trip to Beirut, where at the time Edwin Wilson and Frank Terpil were running an assassin training school, Mark Chapman took a position in Fort Chaffee, Arkansas. Chapman worked with Vietnamese refugees.

According to author Fenton Bresler, Chapman had a lifelong friend, known by the pseudonym Gene Scott, who would make frequent visits. A co-worker told the journalist Craig Unger:

> As soon as Gene arrived, Mark's behavior changed. Mark cleaned his nails for Gene, he put on his clean clothes for Gene, he made telephone calls for Gene. And there was Gene's gun. Mark was so non-violent. He hated guns. I still remember them sitting in the office of the YMCA center at Fort Chaffee, playing with his gun, looking at it, talking about it. It just wasn't like Mark. They started rough-housing, then Gene gave Mark this look. He froze.

In 1976 Chapman left the YMCA and took a position as a security guard at the insistence of Gene Scott. Chapman moved to Honolulu, Hawaii in 1977 and stayed at the YMCA youth hostel. He reportedly contacted a suicide hotline while he was there, and was admitted to the Waikiki Mental Health Clinic.

According to Jim Keith, Hawaii has been noted as the location of a mind control assassination training center in the accounts of several intelligence agency defectors. This marked the second time that

Chapman was in the region of assassination training programs.

In the next years Mark David Chapman traveled the world again, with a letter of introduction as a YMCA staff member. How he managed to pay for his round the world trip is not known, and suspicious—resembling the story of many 'lone nut' assassins who traveled great distances without having the means to finance such travel.

In 1979 Mark Chapman returned to Hawaii and was married. There he became fixated with J.D. Salinger's novel *Catcher in the Rye*. He began seeing a psychiatrist with the complaint of receiving "command hallucinations" which told him to kill John Lennon. Chapman himself has said, "It was almost as if I was on some kind of special mission that I could not avoid."

He went to New York City, and in his hotel room built a lavish shrine composed of a Bible, an expired passport, a Todd Rundgren audio tape, and a Wizard of Oz photo.

Chapman bought another copy of *Catcher in the Rye*, and inscribed it "To Holden Caufield from Holden Caufield. This is my statement." At 5 o'clock p.m. that afternoon John and Yoko emerged from their Dakota apartment. Chapman got the Beatle's autograph. When the couple came back for the evening, at 10:50 p.m., Chapman was waiting with a .38 Special and hollow point ammo—provided by none other than Gene Scott.

Chapman fired five bullets into John Lennon's back. He then threw down his gun and began reading the paperback he had purchased.

Police Lieutenant Arthur O'Connor, who first interrogated Chapman, stated:

> It's possible Mark could have been used by somebody. I saw him the night of the murder. I studied him intensely. He looked as if he could have been programmed. ... That was the way he looked and that was the way he talked. It could have been drugs—and no, we did not test for drugs! It was not standard procedure. But looking back, he could have been either drugged or programmed—or a combination of both.

Mark David Chapman described the murder in this manner:

> If you ever get the chance, go to The Dakota building.

I just love that building ... to think that's where it happened. There was no emotion, there was no anger, there was nothing, dead silence in the brain, dead cold quiet. He walked up, he looked at me, I tell you the man was going to be dead in less than five minutes and he looked at me, I looked at him. He walked past and over again saying 'Do it, do it, do it,' over and over again, saying 'Do it, do it, do it, do it,' like that. I pulled the gun out of my pocket, I handed over to my left hand. I don't remember aiming. I must have done, but I don't remember drawing the bead or whatever you call it. And I just pulled the trigger steady five times.

Chapman pleaded guilty in court after the "voice of God" told him to do so. The plea ended the investigation. And just as with Lee Harvey Oswald, Sirhan Sirhan and James Earl Ray, there would never be a trial. Isn't that convenient?

Sources:

Bernstein, Carl, "The CIA and the Media," *Rolling Stone Magazine*, October 20, 1977
The Catcher in the Rye: Reflections [Online] Available: http:\\www.geocities.com/ad_container/pop.html?cuid=9527&keywords=fiction
Channel 2000—The Assassination of RFK [Online] Available: http:\\www.channel2000.com/news/specialassign/news-specialassignment-970801-002627.html
The Government Psychiatric Torture Site [Online] Available: http:\\www.mk-resistance.com/brady.html
The Government Psychiatric Torture Site [Online] Available: http:\www.mk-resistance.com/ecm_apps.html
Keith, Jim, *Mind Control, World Control*, Adventures Unlimited Press
Lawrence, Lincoln, *Were we Controlled?*
McKenna, Terrance, from a radio interview with Art Bell, April 1, 1999, *Late Night with Art Bell*
Melanson, Professor Philip, *The RFK Assassination*, SPI Books
Pease, Lisa, "CBS and the RFK Case," *Probe* [Online] Available:

http:\\www.webcom.com/ctka/pr398-cbs.html
The RFK assassination—The Crime [Online] Available:
http:\\www.homepages.tcp.co.uk/~dlewis/crime.html

TOP SECRET   MAG CHANNELS ONLY

DEFENSE INTELLIGENCE AGENCY

PSYCHOTRONIC WARFARE: SPIRITUAL ACCESS

Prepared by U.S. Army
Medical Intelligence Office
DST-03447/82/018

TOP SECRET   MAG CHANNELS ONLY

Top: A Defense Intelligence Agency brief on
"Psychotronic Warfare." Bottom: An enlarged
x-ray of a brain implant.

Marshall Applegate, cult leader?

Timothy Leary, fall guy?

Robert Kennedy, cult victim?

CHAPTER THIRTEEN

ALTAR BOYS IN THE TEMPLE OF KONTROL

"Free at last. Keep your emotions down,
keep your emotions down."
—Reverend Jim Jones, from his *Last Testament*

The Liquid Conspiracy has employed millions of persons, directly and indirectly, in its various attempts to create total world control. A multi-purpose product of the LC is the *cult*, and the leaders of these institutions prove invaluable as experimenters and shapers of public opinion.

Think of the dark shadow cast upon the Art Bell talk show when Marshall Applewhite and his Heaven's Gate followers committed mass suicide in their Southern California mansion. During March of 1997, 39 members ate phenobarbital, downed it with vodka and wrapped plastic bags around their heads, in an effort to leave their "earthly containers" and join the "companion ship" traveling with comet Hale-Bopp.

The comet's supposed "companion" was first announced on the radio talk show "Coast to Coast" hosted by Art Bell. There was photographic evidence to support this claim, posted on Art Bell's very popular web site, but the "proof" was later found to be a hoax.

Remote viewers Major Ed Dames and Courtney Brown were guests on "Coast to Coast." Both spoke about "viewing" the comet's companion. Curiously, the web server used by Heaven's Gate to recruit new members was the same server used by the technology defense contractor Science Applications International Corporation (SAIC), allegedly a CIA-run company. SAIC funded remote viewing research on behalf of the CIA.

The young Marshall Applewhite left his family and his college amid accusations of a homosexual affair. He enrolled in the University of St. Thomas, Houston, Texas, but left there in 1970 suffering from depression and auditory hallucinations. He checked into a hospital asking the staff to cure his homosexuality.

According to his sister, Marshall experienced a near death experience during a heart attack at the hospital. Some have speculated that while in this state, Applewhite was activated as a cult leader by an agent of some intelligence organization.

Members of the Heaven's Gate cult claimed to have a "Chip of Recognition" implanted in their skull. The implant allowed them to recognize "Luciferians" when they were encountered.

A nearby neighbor and alleged Heaven's Gate member, Stuart Spiro, was extensively connected to the CIA and British Intelligence. He is purported to have been involved with The October Surprise, which helped Ronald Reagan's presidential campaign in 1980. Spiro and his family were murdered in 1992.

A recent survey showed that no event enjoyed as much world-wide recognition as "Jonestown." Ninety-eight percent of persons asked the world over, were knowledgeable of the event in which Reverend Jim Jones and his People's Temple followers committed mass suicide. The Jonestown Massacre left nearly one thousand people dead. A wealth of research indicates that there were unseen forces influencing the cult. According to mind control researchers, "Jonestown was without a doubt an MKULTRA project."

The Rev. Jones had a history of intelligence connections. His lifelong friend Dan Mitrione was trained in the CIA-financed International Police Academy. In 1961, Jones traveled to Brazil, accompanied by Mitrione. According to researcher Michael Meiers, Jones was "working closely with the CIA at that point."

While Jones was living in Brazil, he explained to his neighbors that he was a member of Navy Intelligence. Jones was known to make frequent trips to Belo Horizonte, the home base of CIA operations in Brazil.

Jones returned to the United States in 1963 and set up shop in Ukiah, California. Jones founded his People's Temple and raised funding while rubbing elbows with the pillars in the community. A large contributor, the Layton family, was tied to the conspiracy-run I.G. Farben industrial monolith.

In the late 1970s, because of political fallout from seven mysterious deaths linked to the People's Temple, Jim Jones moved

156

the operation to the jungles of Guyana. He brought his war chest of cash and set up camp with his faithful.

The Jonestown compound was more like a prison than a utopia. Most of the camp, 90 percent women and 80 percent black, lived under slave labor conditions. Transgressions were punished by torture, beatings, and public rape.

Some People's Temple members reported visits from the Nazi butcher Dr. Josef Mengele, who has also been spoken of by many mind control survivors as having been one of the hidden powers lurking behind MKULTRA.

The suicide coincided with a visit from Congressman Leo Ryan. Ryan was an active investigator of CIA abuses. Ryan introduced legislation to transfer the supervision of the CIA from the Armed Forces Committee—known for turning a blind eye to the abuses of the Agency—to the International Relations Committee of the House and the Senate.

It is said that Ryan uncovered information which connected the CIA to the creation of mind control cults. He specifically found CIA links to the Moonies, and the Symbionese Liberation Army which kidnaped Patty Hearst.

Congressman Ryan was shot dead on the airstrip in Port Kaituma, near Jonestown. He was boarding a plane returning from the compound to the States with a Jonestown defector and several journalists. They were attacked by People's Temple guards who reportedly acted like "zombies" according to witnesses.

The suicides began shortly after, though in fact many of the "suicides" were murders according to the initial findings of Dr. Mootoo, the officiating pathologist. The pathologist was the first medical person on the scene. He reported finding fresh needle marks on the majority of the victims. Some of the people had been shot. Some were strangled.

The gun which Jones allegedly used to kill himself was found 200 feet from his body. Jim Jones may have survived the incident. The corpse identified as his did not have his tattoos. In fact, the body was so decomposed that it was unrecognizable.

In all, only 17 American casualties were positively identified. While there were at least 200 survivors of the incident, they have never been contacted by the press.

Congressman Leo Ryan's attorney Joe Holsinger wrote:

The more I investigate the mysteries of Jonestown, the more I am convinced there is something sinister behind it all. There is no doubt in my mind that Jones had very close CIA connections. At the time of the tragedy, the Temple had three boats in the water off the coast. The boats disappeared shortly afterwards. Remember, Brazil is a country that Jones is very familiar with. He is supposed to have money there. And it is not too far from Guyana. My own feeling is that Jones was ambushed by CIA agents who then disappeared in the boats. But the whole story is so mind boggling that I'm willing to concede he escaped with them.

Orders were sent from the President's National Security Advisor to the military to remove "all politically sensitive papers and forms of identification" from the bodies of the Jonestown victims.

Mind control cults exist the world over, teeming with intelligence affiliation.

Followers of the Unification Church of Reverend Sun Myung Moon, are notorious for recruiting at airports. Sun Myung Moon spread his empire from Korea to Japan and the United States, operating a multitude of businesses as Moonie fronts. Moon has spent millions acquiring the University of Bridgeport in Connecticut.

The Unification Church has four members which hold prominent positions in the South Korean Central Intelligence Agency.

The Ukraine doomsday cult The White Brotherhood, and a multinational Rosicrucian-Templar offshoot cult The Sovereign Order of the Solar Temple have created quite a stir in European circles with official government pardons and mystery million dollar payoffs. The Solar Temple was another site of a mass "suicide."

In 1993, back in the States, the Bureau of Alcohol Tobacco and Firearms (ATF) was attempting to arrest Branch Davidian cult leader David Koresh on weapons possession charges. Initially, Koresh was served with a warrant for his arrest at his "Mount Carmel" compound. The service was actually a paramilitary style invasion of the religious group's Waco, Texas compound. The ATF went so far as to enlist the aid of helicopter gun ships. There was an exchange of gunfire, and the agents of the ATF retreated without having taken the cult leader into custody.

The botched invasion led the ATF to bring in the FBI. For over 50 days the U.S. government held a siege on a people who by all appearances were living a quiet, peaceful life. This siege included blaring the Nancy Sinatra song "These Boots are Made for Walkin'" at all hours of the night. Television reception was also jammed for the inhabitants, cutting them off from the rest of the world.

On April 19th, the FBI led a second invasion on the Davidians, this time with armored tanks. As a result of a gas used by the FBI, which they claim was tear gas, the compound caught fire. Approximately 80 men, women, and children were killed. The compound was completely destroyed.

Why was the government interested in wiping out a seemingly insignificant group of strange apocalyptic believers? Why wasn't Koresh arrested while he was away from Mount Carmel, thus sparing the loss of so much life? Did they need an excuse to destroy the compound? Was there something there that they didn't want us to find?

The famous assassins of our time have links to mind control cults as well, raising suspicions that cults may be used to produce programmable killers.

World Vision is an ominous organization. According to the reports of researchers, the church/televangelist outfit was funded primarily by the CIA. During the Vietnam War period the money was funneled through USAID (which still is on record today as contributing five percent of the church's budget). World Vision collected intelligence data in Southeast Asia under the guise of missionary work.

World Vision contacted Jim Jones in Ukiah, California and assisted him with setting up his compound in Guyana. After the massacre, World Vision attempted to move a population in Dominica to Jonestown. The inhabitants of Jonestown today are Laotian refugees from the CIA's secret war with Laos and Cambodia.

If we check the World Vision roster from this period, we learn that the chairman of the board was none other than John Hinckley, Sr. The plot thickens when it is learned that John Lennon's assailant Mark David Chapman "found Jesus" with World Vision. Remember that he worked as a missionary with Vietnamese refugees.

John Hinckley, Jr., the would-be assassin of President Reagan, said that he met "Son of Sam" serial killer David Berkowitz. Berkowitz, who terrorized New York City, was a known to be a member of the cult known as the Process Church.

Cult figure and convicted killer Charles Manson is said to have been an acolyte in the Process Church. Manson is now incarcerated at the state mental hospital in Vacaville, California, where Sirhan Sirhan once received treatment and Dr. Timothy Leary conducted CIA-financed LSD trials.

Throughout the world, the conspiracy has used cults as secret mind control centers. You have read about a few of them, but cult watch groups indicate that there are hundreds of known active cults. Of most we know nothing. Their leaders are destined to become media figures when it is deemed useful, the followers caught like flies in a web of inescapable madness.

This thesis once again returns us to the Illuminated principle *ordo ab chao,* that is, *order from chaos.* The LC uses the religious cults to create chaos which in turn they control. Under the veil of disorder, a killer is born. Just another part of the grand experiment to perfect world domination—with you in the petri dish.

Sources:

Assassination as a Tool of Fascism [Online] Available:
    http:\\www.shout.net/~bigred/assfas
"Close Encounters with the Fourth Reich," *The Ever-Greener,*
    November 8, 1994
Fire from the Sky [Online] Available:
    http:\\www.area51.icom.net/ufo/Majestic_12/firesky2.txt
Keith, Jim, *Mind Control, World Control,* Adventures Unlimited
    Press
Krawcyzk, Glenn, "The New Inquistition: Cult Awareness or the
    Cult of Intelligence?," Part 2, *Nexus,* December 1994
Meiers, Michael, *Was Jonestown a CIA Medical Experiment? A
    Review of the Evidence*
Vasil, Reuben, "Web of Death," *Newsweek Magazine,* April 7, 1997

CHAPTER FOURTEEN

OHIO: STATE OF THE CONSPIRACY

Many eyes watching the conspiracy have been focused on Southern Nevada, at the top-secret military base known only as Area 51. But what if the federal government had established, for its Black Ops, an entire State? This may sound ridiculous on the surface, but haven't many of the conspiracy's schemes seemed unthinkable? Lets us consider that the State of Ohio may in fact be a legal cloak concealing a growing monster.

Most Americans are knowledgeable that the Constitution requires that a person who becomes President must be a citizen of the United States. Few know, however, that at one time in our history a man served as President who was not even a citizen—*technically*. The man was William Taft, the 27th President. His Presidency was not wholly remarkable, and many of the changes occurring during his term have gone unnoticed.

Taft, not an American citizen? You see, William Taft was born in 1857 in the State of Ohio. Only, Ohio wasn't really a State.

Ohio met all of the requirements for Statehood in 1803, but Congress did not approve Ohio's application at the time. Ohio wasn't admitted into the Union until 1953, when Congress made its admission retroactive. However, an ensuing problem is that the Constitution prohibits the Congress from passing retroactive legislation.

It gets a bit hairier as a legal problem. After serving as President of the United States, Taft was later appointed as Chief Justice of the Supreme Court. So because Taft was not a citizen, everything he

163

had done in his career as President and Chief Justice would legally become null and void. To avoid a Constitutional crisis, the courts have refused to discuss the entire issue, referring concerned citizens to address the matter with Congress, which in turn has refused to approach the matter.

Technicalities? So what? Well, *technically* under Taft's Presidency was born the Federal Income Tax!

President William Taft was the son of Alphonso Taft, who in 1833 co-founded the secret order of the Skull and Bones at Yale University. The Skull and Bones boys founded the Council on Foreign Relations, with the aid of Cecil Rhodes' Round Table. The society basically funded the Bolshevik revolution.

President George Bush is perhaps the most famous member of the Skull and Bones. I hope you are starting to see how the dots connect.

For one hundred fifty years the State of Ohio was not that at all. This would have given the conspiratorial forces plenty of time to plant the seeds of a secret government without any inconvenience of having to follow the law—*technically*.

Right now, strange things are afoot in the State of Ohio. NASA has recently involved itself in anti-gravity research. They have endorsed the work of Russian scientist Podkletnov, who reportedly reduced the effect of gravity by two percent while rapidly spinning a superconductive ceramic disk inside a container of super-cold liquid nitrogen. The objects placed above the disk showed a small drop in weight. Thus, Podkletnov's disk may act as a gravity shield.

The NASA Marshall Research Center has attempted on numerous occasions to duplicate the experiment without avail. And though no other researchers have been able to replicate Podkletnov's results, NASA has contracted a Columbus, Ohio firm by the name of Superconductive Components to do just that.

Podkletnov's experiments have fallen under severe criticism in the field of physics, but NASA, amidst recent serious budget cuts, persists in efforts to validate the "mad scientist's" hypothesis. Why?

If you ask Ohio UFO researcher Rene Soderbeck, he'll tell you. "For a long time now the government has been attempting to reverse engineer UFOs here in Ohio. Like [Col. Philip] Corso says, much of what we attribute to modern technology actually resulted from UFO reverse engineering. They've [NASA] been able to crudely reproduce the anti-gravity technology, but now they want to know how it works."

Soderbeck's claims that the government is conducting reverse

164

engineering in Ohio are congruent with statements by former NSC scientist Dr. Michael Wolf. Wolf claims that the United States Navy first recovered an extraterrestrial craft which had crashed in the ocean off the coast of San Diego, California. The craft and the dead alien bodies within were secretly taken to the Foreign Technology Section at Wright Patterson Air Force Base in Dayton, Ohio. They were subsequently studied by the Retfours Special Studies Group.

Each day, NASA receives dozens of proposals from fringe scientists. Why have they invested money into Podkletnov's ideas? Because they know how it works, now they want to know why.

The LC isn't limiting its scientific inquiries in Ohio to anti-gravity development. Far more disturbing is evidence suggesting biological experimentation, producing horrible results. It is public knowledge that there are a number of genetic engineering projects currently underway at the University of Ohio, might there be a hidden biological project underway? Forget about Dulce, monsters are lurking in Ohio.

In January of 1995, Joedy Cook was hiking near Akron, Ohio and happened upon an unusual structure, obviously made by some sort of being for protection against the elements. The structure consisted of large branches forming a sort of tunnel, covered over with smaller branches and then covered with other forest material and grass. Cook has come to call these structures "nests." Typically there is a lingering odor within the nest, and hairs have been found on the floor.

When Cook questioned the locals about the nests he was told they were built by a creature known as the "Grassman." Sightings are said to go back years.

In all, Cook has discovered nine of these structures with the aid of his associate, George Clappison. Cook and Clappison published their reports in various media which eventually led to a phone call from a man who identified himself as a U.S. Army Colonel.

The Colonel, who has asked that his name be withheld, explained that the Army has instructions to seek out and destroy the nests which they officially term "birthing complexes." The Colonel went on to explain that the tunnels were part of an extensive Cold War emergency shelter system.

When the tunnels were originally excavated, in secret to avoid public alarm, the bones of gorilla-like beings were uncovered. Furthermore, the intact bodies of six unidentified beings were recovered, as well as a placenta—which led to the term birthing complexes.

The truth may be stranger than fiction. Some researchers have indicated that the U.S. Army's Grassman is evidence of an early bio-experiment gone wrong, hence the government's interest in destroying them. I have heard audio recordings of the creature and they are both frightening and convincing.

Grassman is not the only unusual beast roaming the Ohio countryside. The accounts of two policemen describe an abnormal reptilian which has come to be known as the Loveland Creature.

Early on the morning of March 3, 1972, Officer Williams was driving toward Loveland. He was driving cautiously because of ice on the road. He saw what looked like a dog by the side of the road. Williams slowed his car to avoid hitting the animal. As he stopped the car, the animal stood up immediately, on two feet. It looked at him for a moment and then leaped over a guard rail into the Little Miami River.

The Loveland Creature is described as 3 to 4 feet tall, weighing maybe 50 to 75 pounds. Its body looked leathery, and its head resembled a frog or a lizard. Williams made no official record of his sighting, though he did let the dispatcher know what he has seen. He returned later that morning with another officer who confirmed that something had left a "scraping trail" on its way down to the river.

A couple of weeks went by before the creature was spotted again. An Officer Johnson was driving from Loveland on the same road as Williams had driven. He spotted what appeared to be something dead in the middle of the road. He got out of his car to put the animal on the roadside until the game warden could come to pick up the carcass. As he leaned out his door, the creature that he thought was dead rose to its feet, and began to half-walk and half-bobble over to the guard rail. Instead of making a dive for the river though, this time the Loveland Creature lifted one leg at a time over the rail, keeping its eyes upon the policeman.

Johnson took a shot at the animal, missing his mark as it disappeared into the river below.

The creature was also seen by an area farmer that same month. Might the Loveland Creature have been another experiment gone wrong?

MKULTRA survivor Lynne Moss-Sharman describes an account with "Frogman" while she was tortured at Colgate College by Dr. Ewen Cameron, under CIA Sub Project 68. Where did "Frogman" come from? Sharman describes a host of other mutants she was with

166

during her ordeal, which I briefly covered previously.

There is no shortage of mysterious monster sightings in Ohio. In 1978 the residents of Butler, Ohio reported sightings of a seven foot tall humanoid creature with an enormous head and large red eyes. It emitted a foul odor and a terrifying scream.

In 1977 two boys near Eaton, Ohio encountered a nine foot ape-like creature. The sighting was said to coincide with nearby cattle mutilations.

One cannot consider the ring of secret government bases such as Area 51, S4, and Dulce, without including in the discussion Wright Patterson Air Force Base. Beneath the Air Force base in Dayton, Ohio is hidden the underground base S3. S3, according to a multitude of accounts by whistle blowers, is where the United States is storing most of its recovered UFOs. As recently as September 1989, according to researcher John Ford, the U.S. government was sending extraterrestrial crafts to S3 for storage and research.

[As a side note: John Ford, founder of the Long Island UFO Network, became a thorn in the side of local authorities. After he repeated his accusations of government UFO cover-up, he was imprisoned on trumped up charges, ironically, charged with conspiracy.]

Unlike most politicians, the late Senator Barry Goldwater had a healthy interest in UFOs. Goldwater was a retired Air Force Reserve Brigadier General and pilot. In an amazingly straightforward display, he once asked General Curtis Lamay if he could visit the "Blue Room" at Wright Patterson where, Goldwater claims, he was told physical evidence existed confirming the existence of alien aircraft. The Senator quoted Lamay's response as, "Hell no, you can't go. I can't go, and don't ask me again."

What material could be so secret that our top elected officials are not permitted access to it? This is a question that hundreds of thousands of UFO witnesses are asking.

But another question that we should all be asking is—what is going on in Ohio?

Sources:

Grassman [Online] Available:
    http:\\www.users1.ee.net/pmason/grassman3.html
High in the Middle and Round on Both Ends [Online] Available:

http://parascope.com/

NASA homepage [Online] Available: http:\\www.nasa.gov

Podkletnov—Gravity Page [Online] Available:
   http:\\www.rbbi.com/folders/tech/basic/gravity.html

Skull and Bones [Online] Available:

   http:\\www.geocities.com/ad_container/pop.html?cuid=9623&k
   eywords=none

Superconductive Components [Online] Available:
   http:\\www.superconductive.com

UFO quotes [Online] Available:
   http:\\www.connect.net/mattvest/govtqts.html

CHAPTER FIFTEEN

AIDS: PREFAB WORLD PLAGUE

"Depopulation should be the highest priority of U.S. foreign policy
towards the Third World."
—from the declassified National Security Memorandum 200,
written by Henry Kissinger

AIDS, the Acquired Immune Deficiency Syndrome, is spreading
across the planet like wildfire. Over nine million people have died
from this contagious illness which attacks the immune system itself.
AIDS leaves its victim defenseless against disease and infection.

The illness is caused by HIV, the Human Immunodeficiency Virus,
which is spread through exposure to the body fluids of a carrier.
Predominantly, AIDS is spread through promiscuous sexual
behavior, which increases likelihood of exposure. AIDS is also
rampant among intravenous drug users, spread through sharing
needles.

HIV seems custom designed to target people engaged in certain
supposedly immoral behavior. Like the Wrath of God, as some
fundamentalist have suggested. The fact is though, aside from
homosexuals and heroin addicts, AIDS has infected millions in
underdeveloped third world countries. There is growing evidence
that AIDS is a man-made disease.

In an excerpt from the Senate Library report of an appropriations
hearing before the United States Subcommittee on Department of
Defense from the Ninety First Congress, first session, the
development of a "synthetic biological agent" was discussed. The
1969 report indicates that within a five to ten year period, it would
be possible to develop an agent which "does not naturally exist and

for which no natural immunity could have been acquired."

Congressman Sikes of Florida is on record inquiring what the advantages of such a development program would be. The report concludes by disclosing that the matter of initiating such a program through the National Academy of Sciences—National Research Council was discussed, but the reluctance of the Committee to involve the NAS-NRC in such a "controversial endeavor" led to the two-year postponement of said program. In 1970 the program received ten million dollars in funding.

Hardest hit by the AIDS epidemic are the peoples of Central Africa. So much so, that the region is now referred to as the "AIDS belt." In 1972 the World Health Organization (WHO) administered smallpox vaccinations to thousands in this region.

Coincidentally, or perhaps not so coincidentally, the first outbreak of AIDS followed the immunizations. The *London Times* reported it with headlines on the front page of its May 11, 1987 edition.

Dr. Strecker, the world's leading investigative authority in the man-made origins of AIDS, claims that the disease was developed in the lab (quoted verbatim):

> ... we believe the fact that the AIDS virus was not a natural phenomena but a phenomena that resulted as a result of a laboratory manipulation. In other words, AIDS came out of the laboratory, it didn't come out of the generals of Africa or out on some strange black source in Africa or some other abhorrent sexual characteristics of Africans. But it came directly out of the laboratory and we believe that we can trace it to the results of work in laboratories at the United States National Institute of Health as well as particular laboratories in New Orleans and Louisiana area.

A Hepatitis B vaccine was given to several thousand male homosexuals in the cities of New York and San Francisco. Every one of these individuals contracted AIDS. This is the first known American outbreak of the disease, and the commonality between the victims was this specific vaccination. The fact is well documented, but never discussed in the mainstream media.

An expose of drug trafficking by the CIA, reported in the *San Jose Mercury News*, coupled with recent revelations regarding the Tuskegee Syphilis experiments, have brought calls of concern from

172

the black community regarding the AIDS epidemic. According to an October 6, 1996 Associated Press report, "Some believe AIDS, which kills minorities at disproportionately high rates, is a manmade disease designed to keep down the black population."

Author and medical doctor Alan Cantwell takes the assertion one step further in his book *Queer Blood: The Secret AIDS Genocide Plot.* Cantwell debunks the "green monkey" theory of AIDS, namely that the genesis of the disease was probably from a monkey bite or other simian contact, and explains how AIDS began as a covert genocide experiment, using gays and blacks as guinea pigs.

Dr. Cantwell says the theory is not "a paranoid fantasy" and further states:

> It is commonly believed, particularly in the Black community, that AIDS is a secret government genocide plot to eliminate 'undesirables.' The major media never mention books written on the subject of AIDS as manmade, nor will they quote physicians, like myself and others, who publicly promote this idea.

And of course, the conspiracy is highly interested in keeping alternative AIDS theories silenced. In a rare instance, the U.S. Government reverted to bold censorship—book burning. On December 29, 1991, in a move reminiscent of Ray Bradbury's *Fahrenheit 451,* a New York federal court ordered the destruction of all copies of the book *Why We Will Never Win the War on AIDS,* written by Bryan Ellison and Peter Duesberg.

And if the *government* had its way, you would never even know that the book existed.

Sources:

Conspiracy Nation (#7 vol,. 23)
Dark Conspiracies [Online] Available:

http:\\www.sirius.com/~tromine/DarkConspiracies/SomeCons ider.html
Hearings before a Subcommittee of the Committee on Appropriations, House of Representatives, Ninety-First Congress First Session, Part 5, United States Senate Library,

Tuesday July 1, 1969
Kissinger, Henry, National Security Memorandum
Kasset, Michael, Network 23 Television Program
Strecker, Dr. Robert, "Stealth Virus Encephalopathy," from a
lecture given March 9, 1997

The frog boy of Ohio.

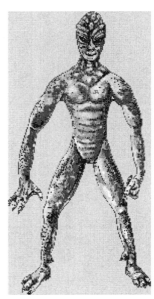

Left, and above: Lizard men as depicted on the Internet. Aliens, or experiments gone horribly wrong?

CHAPTER SIXTEEN

APOCALYPSE NOW: BAR CODES AND BLACK HELICOPTERS

"It's the end of the world as we know it, and I feel fine."
—the rock and roll group R.E.M.

If you've ever subscribed to cable television, you're sure to have seen any number of televangelists ranting about the apocalypse. These doomsday preachers seem to capitalize on the anxieties of modern man by drawing comparisons between the Bible book Revelations and current events, then soliciting donations to feed the fire.

The End Times faction is not exclusively Christian, and as the new millennium approaches even New Agers are jumping on the bandwagon. People such as Gordon-Michael Scallion, with his *Earth Changes Map* can be found painting a whiter shade of a pale horse.

If you've ever listened to the popular radio talk show host Art Bell, then you should be acquainted with "The Quickening," Art Bells term for the apparent speeding up of events around the world—leading to some unseen culmination. Art Bell's talk show *Coast to Coast* is perhaps the largest forum for discussion of the unknown, save the Internet.

Art Bell frequently hosts guests who present end-of-the-world scenarios. Popular guest Major Ed Dames, a remote viewer, is one man who seems to come up with a new demise for civilization every few months.

Another of Bell's guests is favorite Sean David Morton, Ufologist turned seer. Morton, previously a tour guide to Area 51, also entertains us with predictions of catastrophe. According to his vision, in 1998 the Jet Stream was to lower to ground level, causing horrible destructive winds.

Actually, for years guests on the Art Bell show have foreseen the looming demise of the human race. Let us not forget the Hale-Bopp Comet's companion hoax, which left egg on the faces of a number of supposedly reputable researchers.

While some of this can be dismissed as amusing, we must ask what purpose the propagation of unsubstantiated paranoia serves? It may well be true that there have always existed doomsayers, but at no period in history have so many profited so much. Perhaps we should ask who profits the most from this constant undercurrent of paranoia that is festering just below our surface.

The force which seeks to control every mind in the world is the LC. Kilder relayed his knowledge of the LC's plan to exploit the apocalyptic visions of the world's major religions in various statements (directly quoted):

- Through subtle channels, the conspiracy will suggest the environment of a Rapture. They will manufacture famine. They will use the media to hasten a state of immorality in civilization.
- Men and women will gradually surrender their sexual identities in respect to attaining the ideal unisex state which the media are already beginning to portray. Male role models are increasingly effeminate: with long hair, hairless bodies, and developed chests.
- Girls are encouraged to be more aggressive, and popular icons are often bisexual, with their conquests including men and women.
- There will be an appearance of ethical demise, and an increased fascination with the macabre. The apparent world will fit nicely into any apocalyptic framework.

"These are not predictions," Kilder writes. "These are the weapons of a dark conspiracy against mankind. None of what is happening is undesigned."

Kilder insisted that no major catastrophic incident would occur.

178

That would be ineffective. The LC's plan is to keep the world in a state of subtle panic while secretly making us into their slaves. Using every turn to strip another one of our freedoms from us, rights which we will willingly hand over. Confusion reigns. Fear is control, and out of chaos comes order. Kilder believed that the primary purpose for the apocalyptic visions which seemingly now rule the airwaves was for psychological manipulation of the Tavistock Institute variety.

Not that it is the author's opinion that there is nothing to fear. Quite contrary. We shouldn't fear the sky falling, but rather we should fear those who make it appear that the sky is falling. Because it does appear that "the end" is near, and someone *somewhere* has a dark sense of humor.

According to a *USA Today* article from June 11, 1997, a large group of protesters, including more than one thousand clergy, gathered outside Parliament in Athens Greece to demonstrate their opposition to Greek participation in a European Union (EU) program to remove border controls. The program requires that every citizen be issued an EU identity card. The point of contention is the content of the card. Everyone will be issued a bar code number, which will include the number 666 in its design.

"666" is recognized among Christians as the Mark of the Beast. The Book of Revelations in the New Testament of the Holy Bible makes the case like this:

> Also it causes all, both small and great, both rich and poor, both free and slave, to be marked on the right hand or the forehead, so that no one can buy or sell unless he has the mark, that is, the name of the beast or the number of its name. This calls for wisdom: let him who has understanding reckon the number of the beast for it is a human number, its number is six hundred and sixty-six. (Rev. 13:16-18)

The number 666 appearing in bar codes is nothing new. Just about anything that you purchase has a UPC bar code. It's the series of lines that the cashier scans to get the price to ring up on the register. If you'll bear with me, I will point out the Mark of the Beast to you.

Each line in the code, or each set of lines, stands for a digit between one and ten. Note that two thin lines next to one another represent the number six. Most of the lines will have a digit beneath them, except for three sets which never have a digit printed beneath them. Look at a few different bar codes; you will find that there is one common sequence in all of them. The beginning, middle, and last set of lines have no digits. These unmarked sets are always the UPC symbol representing the digit six. Always. Hence, the Mark of the Beast is on everything that you buy. Check it out for yourself!

Now this is very unlikely a coincidence. Which leaves two possible scenarios: (1) Satan is ruling the planet Earth, or (2) the UPC bar code system was intentionally designed to suggest that Satan may be running the show.

I will propose that the latter is most likely, though in many ways both answers probably apply.

In order to obtain a UPC bar code for your product, you would have to go through the UCC (Uniform Code Council, Inc.) The UCC operations center is located in Dayton, Ohio. Currently the Board of Governors for the UCC includes executives from several top ranking executives from Fortune 500 companies.

One office is held by the Quaker Oats Company. In late December 1997, the Quaker Oats Company and the Massachusetts Institute of Technology (which has abundant ties to the CIA) settled a lawsuit in which they were charged with having fed radioactive cereal to mentally retarded schoolboys, aged 12 to 17 years, at the Fernald School in Waltham, Massachusetts.

The boys and their families were the unwitting subjects of radiation experiments which took place in the 1940s and 1950s. The boys were told that they were joining a "science club." The members of this club were given extra portions of milk, and taken out to baseball games. They were treated to dinners at restaurants and daytrips to the beach. They were also fed radioactive cereal.

Quaker Oats denies any wrongdoing, despite the offer of settlement. Fortune 500 companies can do that.

So the same people putting radioactive material in mentally retarded kids' cereal are issuing the Mark of the Beast on every product sold. Is this simply a coincidence, a bad joke, or something more clever? The Liquid Conspiracy may well intentionally spread paranoia, and hide it right in front of our eyes.

The drive of world powers to require a universal identification program is nothing to balk at. The EU card is a mild infringement on personal liberty compared to the proposed ID chip program.

Ronald Kane, vice president of the hi-tech control systems company Cubic Corporation, remarks, "If we had our way, we'd implant a chip behind everyone's ear in the maternity ward."

In the book *Project Lucid*, Christian fundamentalist author and researcher Texe Marrs addresses the issue of implantable ID chips. While addressing a hi-tech conference sponsored by IBM, Marrs quotes a top White House Official as saying, "The smart card is a wonderful idea, but even better would be a chip in your ear. We need to go beyond the narrow conceptualization of the smart card and really use some of the technology that's out there."

The ID chip concept may be the link between modern computer technology and the work of mind control madman/pioneer Jose Delgado. *The Wall Street Journal* reports a story that in a U.S. naval research laboratory, experiments have succeeded in uniting living brain cells with microchips.

The hi-tech industry itself may be a tool of creating the apocalypse. Let's look at the firm Lucent Technologies, an AT&T spawned company, located at 666 Fifth St. in New York City. The company offered a press release displaying their new corporate logo, a rough-edged red circle which to some occultists represents a Satanic deity. A recent product development from Lucent is titled "Inferno."

The applications for Inferno are written in a new programming language called Limbo. The dark sense of humor persists ...

The sky may not be falling, but there is plenty falling from the sky. Consider the black helicopter phenomenon. The symbol of the black helicopter has become the tongue-in-cheek emblem of the conspiracy. Hollywood has resourcefully made the black choppers to represent the mysterious secret government in numerous recent films including *Conspiracy Theory, Independence Day*, and *Face Off* —to name a few. While the public may be being desensitized to the image, the black helicopter represents the wings of the monster living among us.

I can attest to having seen one of these aircraft myself. While the current President was making a campaign visit to my hometown, I was walking in a local park. A black, unmarked helicopter flew overhead. It was about 300 feet above the ground. I could see two men inside, and gunnery on the underside. I am not personally familiar enough with modern military aircraft to identify the type. All that I can say was that the incident convinced me of their reality.

There are actually thousands of accounts of black helicopter sightings. Many can be found on Internet newsgroups. Their purpose can only be a matter of speculation, since the United States government officially denies their existence.

In a letter to *The Independent*, New Mexico resident Sheryl Hines writes that black helicopters sprayed an "unusual liquid" over her rural property. Animals suffered a number of ailments, including hair loss, distemper, and lesions.

Sightings of black helicopters in New Mexico, and in other states, have coincided with mysterious cattle mutilations. Typically these mutilated animals are marked with fluorescent paint, which may aid identification in the night. Furthermore, the cattle have been found to be injected with a harmful bacteria called Clostridium. The Church Senate Select Committee on Intelligence in 1970 found that the CIA had stockpiled this same bacteria.

Another purpose for the mutilations could be *blood harvesting*. Science has recently proven that bovine hemoglobin, with the aid of a special purification system, could be a substitute for human blood in cases of "unforeseen national emergencies."

Some have speculated that the black helicopters represent a move toward a New World Order, and that the lack of insignias appearing on aircraft is actually a preparation toward putting the United States military under UN control. The UN is certainly the army of the New World Order, and more frequently these troops are being housed and trained in the United States. The pilots of the black helicopters are often reported as wearing the UN uniform.

The black helicopters aren't the only sky show going on these days. Perhaps even stranger are the reports of "contrails." These are intersecting vapor trails left by airplanes. It is alleged that the military is spraying chemicals into the atmosphere via these vapor trails. According to contrail expert David Tilbury, spectrometer samples obtained of the intersecting trails indicated the presence of three known pathogens.

"From around the world these reports are coming in of strange aircraft contrails which do not disappear but stretch and linger," informs Tilbury. "This is usually followed by reports of mass illness."

According to an MSNBC report, NASA is photographing the contrails from space. The official line is that they're studying the contrails' effect on weather.

That simply arouses suspicion from researcher Joe Burton. "NBC can produce all the BS they want to on the subject, but I do not have to buy into it," Burton declares. "I immediately learned chemicals and viruses were dropping out of the contrails as they opened up and fanned out. One of the chemicals was EDB, which is added to many petroleum products, highly toxic to humans, animals and plants. The viruses I found were coming from naturally-forming bacteria in the water based fuels. The planes have built-in bladders to hold and spray these toxic clouds."

EDB is a key element of 28 pesticides, and highly poisonous. EDB is heavily regulated by the EPA and has been banned from use for several years.

Burton has been tracking the contrails since April of 1998. He has even reported seeing "electrically charged" contrails. The vapors led him to discover a secret military base hidden deep in the forests of Tennessee. After returning from the site, Burton experienced blood in his urine, and on one occasion, blood gushed from his mouth. These are symptoms resembling Gulf War Syndrome.

Joe Burton visited an M.D. who conducted a full body scan. The physician discovered that several biological agents, including enzyme production inhibiting amino acid poisons, had entered through his lungs and settled in his internal organs.

The scan also found Hepatitis-A, Epstein Barr disease, and the mysterious virus V-2, none of which Burton had previously been known to have encountered. These viruses are laboratory agents. Burton's doctor informed him that if they could not purge these chemicals from his body, he would die within a year.

Burton estimates that the United States government is engaging in biological warfare experiments and weather control experiments at the expense of American lives.

William Wallace, a Washington state resident, became ill with fatigue and diarrhea after spending New Year's Day watching two twin engine jets travel in an east-west grid pattern, crisscrossing the sky with contrails. A neighbor working outside came down with the same symptoms. Neither of the two gentlemen's wives, who both spent the day inside, showed any symptoms.

After going to the press, Wallace says that he was "attacked" by similar planes.

In March 1996, the dentist Dr. Greg Hanford purchased a camera and binoculars to observe planes spraying white bands above his home in Bakersfield, California. Dr. Hanford has counted 40 or 60 jets on some days.

"Everybody seems to be getting sick from it, hackin' and coughin' when you really get nailed with this stuff," says Hanford. Hanford and his receptionist suffered for five months with severe respiratory infections, despite courses of four different antibiotics.

Dr. Hanford has sometimes seen what he terms "furry globular balls" spread downwind in a long feather from the aircraft.

In a striking resemblance to the black helicopter phenomenon, many of the planes sighted spraying unusual contrails have no identifying markings.

Similar accounts are reported in the land down under. On August 11, 1998 *USA Today* newspaper reported that dozens of residents in Quirindi, Australia witnessed "cobwebs" fall from the sky after unidentified aircraft passed overhead.

Another contrail investigator has linked sickness to contrail sightings. The author of *Bringing the War Home*, journalist William Thomas, suggests that outbreaks of the flesh-eating virus, Strep-A coincide with the strange intersecting cloud paths. Thomas has collected chemical analyses of contrail material, data which confirm that dangerous and toxic chemicals, both biological and inorganic, are present.

Don't for a moment believe that the government of the United States wouldn't poison its own people. In the wake of the Human Research Subjects Protections Act of 1997, a number of agencies within the Federal Government have recently revealed their use of American citizens as unwitting subjects in a number of experiments. Under pressure, bureaucracies from the DOE to the CIA have admitted to unethical and non-consensual 'experiments' which have included tests using biological agents, narcotics, and radiation.

Much of the CIA's experimentation has been previously discussed in this book. However, it should be advised that the CIA, though quite prominent and powerful, is but one of dozens of organizations within the United States Government which has confessed to experimenting on the unwitting population.

Though the past actions of the U.S. government may portend a guilty conscience, its current behavior suggests otherwise. This behavior is, in fact, perfectly within U.S. law. Under Title 50 of the U.S. Code, Chemical and Biological Warfare Program, Section 1520:

> (1) The Secretary of Defense may not conduct any test or experiment involving the use of any chemical or biological agent on civilian populations unless local civilian officials in the area in which the test or experiment is to be conducted are notified in advanced of such test or experiment, and such test or experiment may then be conducted only after the expiration of the thirty

day period beginning on the date of such notification.

Note that the military need only *notify* local civilian officials before conducting tests on the population. Also, the term "local civilian officials" is disturbingly vague.

From the sky to the water, there may be no refuge from the conspiracy's poison rain. Just as we need the air we breathe, we need the water we drink. And the conspiracy has been tainting our drinking water since 1945. How have they done it? Under the guise of promoting the health of our children! The United States Government has sold us fluoride like it was snake oil.

According to the American Dental Association (ADA), "Water fluoridation remains the safest, most effective and most economical public health measure to reduce tooth decay, and there has not been any evidence that shows a relationship between fluoridation and other diseases in humans."

Proponents have labeled fluoridation opponents as "paranoid." Fortunately, the rest of the planet Earth hasn't seen things the same way. Fluoridation has not been allowed in the nations of Belgium, Sweden, Denmark, Holland, France, Italy, or Norway! Are these countries populated by paranoids? Or might there at least be room for an inquiry into the truth about fluoride?

On January 25, 1945 the U.S. began adding fluoride to drinking water in Grand Rapids, Michigan. The official reason was to prevent tooth decay on a mass scale. But what else does fluoride do to the body?

Evidence suggests that fluoride increases the risk of certain cancers, accelerates the aging process, decreases fertility, causes damage to the kidneys, and impairs vital DNA repair enzymes which are crucial to the immune system. All this risk occurs even at the one part per million recommended concentration in drinking water.

According to Dr. John Yiamouyiannis, author of *Fluoride: The Aging Factor*, between 30,000 and 50,000 deaths a year can be attributed to fluoridation. Studies dating back to 1963 performed by the American Academy of Science indicate that fluoridation results in a marked increase in melanotic tumors.

If the concern is so high regarding fluoride, then why are so many communities fluoridating their water supplies? In 1942, the United States Public Health Service, a division (curiously) of the United States Treasury Department, legislated the safe level of fluoridation acceptable in drinking water to be 1 ppm. The chief officer of the

Treasury was Andrew Mellon, coincidentally also the owner of Alcoa. Would there be any more convenient and cost-effective a way to dispose of this toxic byproduct of Sodium Fluoride than by selling it to public utilities to add to drinking water?

But that motive may serve only as a cover for the multilayered conspiracy. Because what fluoride does to the body is secondary to its effect on the brain. You may recall that earlier in this book it was told how fluoride was instrumental in the German plans for world domination. Might fluoride be another dark pearl captured from the Nazi war chest?

The Soviets have known the advantages of this chemical mind control agent, having used the substance since the 1940s to turn the population of their vast network of concentration camps into docile sheep.

The earlier in life one begins ingesting sodium fluoride, the more prevalent its contraindications are. Public schools in North America have recently begun instituting regular fluoride treatment programs. Add this to the toothpaste used by children the recommended three times a day, along with food products grown and processed with fluoridated water, and the level of fluoride consumed by our kids is frightening.

If you thought that the perils confronting you in modern life were insurmountable, think of our children. The Liquid Conspiracy is poisoning them, while the parents of this world, and their leaders, turn a blind eye. Are the children of America being transformed into the slaves of the New World Order?

Perhaps the introduction of the metallic compound sodium fluoride into the brain is merely paving the way for a set of instructions to be sent via the conspiracy's most terrifying device as of date: HAARP.

The U.S. government tells us that the High-Frequency Active Auroral Research Program is an "ionospheric heater" designed to heat a portion of the upper atmosphere like a "burrito in a microwave oven," but it's real intention is the subject of controversy.

HAARP can best be described as a large array of antennae remotely located in Alaska. It is a radio transmitter approximately 72,000 times stronger than the largest commercial radio station in the United States. Inspired by the works of Nikola Tesla, the array is capable of a number of radio wonders.

The U.S. Navy plans to use this technology to communicate with submarines at previously unreachable depths. HAARP can do this because it is able to supercharge a radio frequency, and focus it at one specific point. This capability arouses questions about the possible applications for controlling human behavior.

HAARP can broadcast at frequencies identical to those used by the brain. In his book *HAARP: The Ultimate Weapon of the Conspiracy*, author Jerry E. Smith writes:

> While there is no discernible direct connection between the CIA's experimentation with LSD and other drugs in the '50s and '60s and HAARP today, there is a stunning lesson to be learned in the CIA's use of a new technology (LSD) on unwitting subjects within this country. The potential for similar misuse of technology (HAARP) certainly exists today. I very definitely see a parallel between these two programs.

Smith relays in his comprehensive analysis that the intelligence community and the military have an ongoing desire to "win the battle for the minds of men" and that they don't care if they have to "turn 'men' into 'zombies' in order to accomplish this aim." HAARP is owned and managed by the very people who have been on the forefront of this war for decades.

HAARP represents the culmination of electromagnetic brain manipulation research that began with infamous mad scientist Dr. Jose Delgado. Delgado once told the U.S. Congress:

> We need a program of psychosurgery for political control of our society. The purpose is physical control of the mind. Everyone who deviates from the given norm can be surgically mutilated. The individual may think that the most important reality is his own existence, but this is only his personal point of view. This lacks historical perspective. Man does not have the right to develop his own mind. This kind of liberal orientation has great appeal. We must electrically control the brain. Someday armies and generals will be controlled by electric stimulation of the brain.

Despite these outrageous statements made before the Congress of the United States, Delgado received grants financing his research from the Office of Naval Research—which co-directs HAARP.

By no means are the possible applications of HAARP limited to mind control. This multi-tasking weapon is also capable of inflicting catastrophic damage through 'environmental manipulation.' HAARP is able to control weather patterns, creating floods or droughts on command. HAARP may also be used to create earthquakes using Extreme Low Frequencies (ELF).

If the LC was truly going to bring about the artificial apocalypse then HAARP would be the instrument of choice. Imagine a machine with the ability to project religious imagery, such as the likeness of Christ or Mohammed, on the night sky over a particular region. Simultaneously this projection would be accompanied by thoughts of ecstasy or terror beamed into the minds of the people on the ground. To top it off, the weather could be under the complete control of the puppet masters. HAARP is the weapon of ultimate control. And after all is said and done, the LC simply seeks ultimate control.

Sources:

Congressional Record, No.26.,Vol. 118, February 24, 1974 edition.
Fluoride Controversy [Online] Available:
    http:\www.sukel.com/fluoride.html
Hayakawa, Norio F., lecture given on November 16, 1991
Keith, Jim, *Black Helicopters Over America: Strikeforce for the New World Order*, Illuminet Press
Marrs, Texe, *Project L.U.C.I.D.*, Living Truth Ministries
"Protesters: The Devil's in EU Pacts Details," *USA Today*, June 11, 1997
Radioactive Iron Fed to Boys at Fernald School, Waltham, MA [Online] Available:
    http:\www.enviroweb.org/hecweb/archive/nucs/RadioOats.html
Smith, Jerry E., *HAARP: The Ultimate Weapon of the Conspiracy*, Adventures Unlimited Press, 1998
Thomas, William, interview March 17, 1999
Tilbury, David, *Strange Contrails*
UCC commerce [Online] Available: http:\\www.uc-council.org/
Valerian, Valdamar, *Matrix III*, 1992
Yiamouyiannis, Dr. John, *Fluoride: The Aging Factor*

188

EPILOGUE

THE SHAPE OF THINGS TO COME

Before you invest thousands of dollars into building your backyard bunkers, before you check out from the planet and ride a comet, rest assured that world isn't going to end.

Your world will change, though it shall mutate gradually. Your lifestyle will develop into one compatible with the New World Order, and you will surrender your rights gladly, as you will deem the sacrifice noble. Soon, you may even forfeit your individuality as the One World State will assume the role of primary importance. And you shall happily exchange your identity, as a man-created-equal for man-created-servant, as a bride exchanges her name for a kiss.

Who will lead this New World Order? The Secretary General of the United Nations? The President of The United States? Bill Gates? HAL 9000? Will the One World Government be a republic? A technocracy? An oligarchy? The answer to these questions is that the world will be governed by whatever structure is most convenient to the moment. The LC can't set a plan in stone, as it must remain fluid for its survival, and to prevent its exposure.

There probably won't be an alien invasion: the Liquid Conspiracy will simply continue to psychologically torture a select few with abduction experiences. There will be no nuclear war: they will just keep you worrying about it until a more horrible weapon is developed for you to worry about. Nothing so catastrophic as to cause the end of mankind or civilization will ever happen at the hands of the LC. It simply is not their style.

What will *this island Earth* look like in the years to come? Will it be a barren wasteland with exhausted resources? Will it appear as paradise thanks to the marvels of future science? We can't rightly say, but assume that it will appear exactly as the conspirators want it, to serve whatever outcome they desire.

Assume that everything in your life shall and does reflect the intention of the conspiracy: because soon it may be difficult to distinguish your will from theirs.

The reality is that reality is not long for this world. Thanks to the efforts of brilliant scientists coupled with the conspiracy's persistent, unworthy ambitions, technology is near to placing total world control in the hands of a few diabolical people.

The day may come when you wake up to men in blue uniforms marching up your street, confiscating your firearms and dissident literature, and taking your children to education camps as black helicopters blaze overhead, blasting curfew ordinance. But you won't break a sweat.

Similar things have happened; such things will likely occur again. The frightening truth is that just as you have never known the real history of the world, you will not recognize the real present. You will not live in terror or anguish. You will love Big Brother.

If the LC has its way, you will embrace every unfathomable atrocity, and live contentedly as a mind controlled zombie to the New World Order. The world may, by today's standards, be unlivable; but you will adore living in it.

Reaching and maintaining that world is the goal of the conspiracy. Only the question of motive remains. Why? What drives someone to desire such a paradigm?

It must be assumed that like any other person, a conspirator is true to his nature. And that nature is to control others.

Perhaps the nature of the beast is reflective of a grander revelation—that the conspiracy itself is controlled by the mechanics of an even darker force. A force from which there may be only one defense: *prayer.*

The beast that once thrived in the darkness has been illuminated by the courage of a few. The few which carried the torch to shine upon the creature's face in that leaden cavern, though the flames burned, they were steadfast. These noblemen have passed this torch to us. And as we stare bravely at this monster, let us lead it to out into the daylight where in the glory of God's eternal Illumination, the Liquid Conspiracy unmasked shall evaporate and rise to the forgiving embrace of Heaven.

Liquid Conspiracy

JFK, LSD, the CIA, Area 51 & UFOs

by
George Piccard

Mind Control And Conspiracy Series

THE
ADVENTURES
UNLIMITED
CATALOG

PHILOSOPHY & RELIGION

THE CHRIST CONSPIRACY
The Greatest Story Ever Sold
by Acharya S.

In this highly controversial and explosive book, archaeologist, historian, mythologist and linguist Acharya S. marshals an enormous amount of startling evidence to demonstrate that Christianity and the story of Jesus Christ were created by members of various secret societies, mystery schools and religions in order to unify the Roman Empire under one state religion. In developing such a fabrication, this multinational cabal drew upon a multitude of myths and rituals that existed long before the Christian era, and reworked them for centuries into the religion passed down to us today. Contrary to popular belief, there was no single man who was at the genesis of Christianity; Jesus was many characters rolled into one. These characters personified the ubiquitous solar myth, and their exploits were well known, as reflected by such popular deities as Mithras, Heracles/Hercules, Dionysos and many others throughout the Roman Empire and beyond. The story of Jesus as portrayed in the Gospels is revealed to be nearly identical in detail to that of the earlier savior-gods Krishna and Horus, who for millennia preceding Christianity held great favor with the people. *The Christ Conspiracy* shows the Jesus character as neither unique nor original, not "divine revelation." Christianity re-interprets the same extremely ancient body of knowledge that revolved around the celestial bodies and natural forces.

256 PAGES. 6x9 PAPERBACK. ILLUSTRATED. $16.95. CODE: CHRC

THE AQUARIAN GOSPEL OF JESUS THE CHRIST
Transcribed from the Akashic Records
by Levi

First published in 1908, this is the amazing story of Jesus, the man from Galilee, and how he attained the Christ consciousness open to all men. It includes a complete record of the "lost" 18 years of his life, a time on which the New Testament is strangely silent. During this period Jesus travelled widely in India, Tibet, Persia, Egypt and Greece, learning from the Masters, sages and wisemen of the East and the West in their temples and schools. Included is information on the Council of the Seven Sages of the World, Jesus with the Chinese Master Mencius (Meng Tzu) in Tibet, the ministry, trial, execution and resurrection of Jesus.

270 PAGES. 6x9 PAPERBACK. INDEX. $14.95. CODE: AGJC

CONVERSATIONS WITH THE GODDESS
by Mark Amaru Pinkham

Return of the Serpents of Wisdom author Pinkham tells us that "The Goddess is returning!" Pinkham gives us an alternative history of Lucifer, the ancient King of the World, and the Matriarchal Tradition he founded thousands of years ago. The name Lucifer means "Light Bringer" and he is the same as the Greek god Prometheus, and is different from Satan, who was based on the Egyptian god Set. Find out how the branches of the Matriarchy—the Secret Societies and Mystery Schools—were formed, and how they have been receiving assistance from the Brotherhoods on Sirius and Venus to evolve the world and overthrow the Patriarchy. Learn about the revival of the Goddess Tradition in the New Age and why the Goddess wants us all to reunite with Her now! An unusual book from an unusual writer!

296 PAGES. 7x10 PAPERBACK. ILLUSTRATED. BIBLIOGRAPHY. $14.95. CODE: CWTG.

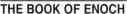

THE BOOK OF ENOCH
The Prophet
translated by Richard Laurence

This is a reprint of the Apocryphal *Book of Enoch the Prophet* which was first discovered in Abyssinia in the year 1773 by a Scottish explorer named James Bruce. In 1821 *The Book of Enoch* was translated by Richard Laurence and published in a number of successive editions, culminating in the 1883 edition. One of the main influences from the book is its explanation of evil coming into the world with the arrival of the "fallen angels." Enoch acts as a scribe, writing up a petition on behalf of these fallen angels, or fallen ones, to be given to a higher power for ultimate judgment. Christianity adopted some ideas from Enoch, including the Final Judgment, the concept of demons, the origins of evil and the fallen angels, and the coming of a Messiah and ultimately, a Messianic kingdom. The *Book of Enoch* was ultimately removed from the Bible and banned by the early church. Copies of it were found to have survived in Ethiopia, and fragments in Greece and Italy.

224 PAGES. 6x9 PAPERBACK. ILLUSTRATED. INDEX. $16.95. CODE: BOE

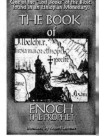

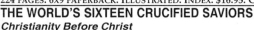

THE WORLD'S SIXTEEN CRUCIFIED SAVIORS
Christianity Before Christ
by Kersey Graves, foreword by Acharya S.

A reprint of Kersey Graves' classic and rare 1875 book on Christianity before Christ, and the 16 messiahs or saviors who are known to history before Christ! Chapters on: Rival Claims of the Saviors; Messianic Prophecies; Prophecies by the Figure of a Serpent; Virgin Mothers and Virgin-Born Gods; Stars Point Out the Time and the Saviors' Birthplace; Sixteen Saviors Crucified; The Holy Ghost of Oriental Origin; Appollonius, Osiris, and Magus as Gods; 346 Striking Analogies Between Christ and Krishna; 25th of December as the birthday of the Gods; more. 45 chapters in all.

436 PAGES. 6x9 PAPERBACK. ILUSTRATED. $19.95. CODE: WSCS

THE DARK SIDE OF CHRISTIAN HISTORY
by Helen Ellerbe

Over a period of almost two millennia, millions of people have been oppressed and brutalized by elements in the Christian church in its attempt to control and contain spirituality. *The Dark Side of Christian History* reveals in painstaking detail the tragedies, sorrows and injustices inflicted upon humanity by the Church. Chapters on Political Maneuvering in Rome; Deciding on Doctrine: Sex, Free Will, Reincarnation and the Use of Force; The Dark Ages; The Inquisition and Slavery; the Witch Hunts; more. "This is simply a book that everyone must sit down and read." —Alice Walker, author of the book *The Color Purple*.

221 PAGES. 6x9 PAPERBACK. ILLUSTRATED. $12.95. CODE: DSCH

24 hour credit card orders—call: 815-253-6390 fax: 815-253-6300
email: auphq@frontiernet.net   www.adventuresunlimitedpress.com   www.wexclub.com

LOST CONTINENTS & THE HOLLOW EARTH
I Remember Lemuria and the Shaver Mystery
by David Hatcher Childress & Richard Shaver

Lost Continents & the Hollow Earth is Childress' thorough examination of the early hollow earth stories of Richard Shaver and the fascination that lost continents and the hollow earth have had for the American public. Shaver's rare 1948 book *I Remember Lemuria* is reprinted in its entirety, and the book is packed with illustrations from Ray Palmer's *Amazing Stories* magazine of the 1940s. Palmer and Shaver told of tunnels running through the earth—tunnels inhabited by the Deros and Teros, humanoids from an ancient spacefaring race that had inhabited the earth, eventually going underground, hundreds of thousands of years ago. Childress discusses the famous hollow earth books and delves deep into whatever reality may be behind the stories of tunnels in the earth. Operation High Jump to Antarctica in 1947 and Admiral Byrd's bizarre statements, tunnel systems in South America and Tibet, the underground world of Agartha, UFOs coming from the South Pole, more.
344 PAGES. 6x9 PAPERBACK. ILLUSTRATED. $16.95. CODE: LCHE

INSIDE THE GEMSTONE FILE
Howard Hughes, Onassis & JFK
by Kenn Thomas & David Hatcher Childress

Steamshovel Press editor Thomas takes on the Gemstone File in this run-up and run-down of the most famous underground document ever circulated. Photocopied and distributed for over 20 years, the Gemstone File is the story of Bruce Roberts, the inventor of the synthetic ruby widely used in laser technology today, and his relationship with the Howard Hughes Company and ultimately with Aristotle Onassis, the Mafia, and the CIA. Hughes kidnapped and held a drugged-up prisoner for 10 years; Onassis and his role in the Kennedy Assassination; how the Mafia ran corporate America in the 1960s; more.
320 PAGES. 6x9 PAPERBACK. ILLUSTRATED. $16.00. CODE: IGF

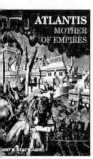

KUNDALINI TALES
by Richard Sauder, Ph.D.

Underground Bases and Tunnels author Richard Sauder on his personal experiences and provocative research into spontaneous spiritual awakening, out-of-body journeys, encounters with secretive governmental powers, daylight sightings of UFOs, and more. Sauder continues his studies of underground bases with new information on the occult underpinnings of the U.S. space program. The book also contains a breakthrough section that examines actual U.S. patents for devices that manipulate minds and thoughts from a remote distance. Included are chapters on the secret space program and a 130-page appendix of patents and schematic diagrams of secret technology and mind control devices.
296 PAGES. 7x10 PAPERBACK. ILLUSTRATED. BIBLIOGRAPHY. $14.95. CODE: KTAL

LIQUID CONSPIRACY
JFK, LSD, the CIA, Area 51 & UFOs
by George Piccard

Underground author George Piccard on the politics of LSD, mind control, and Kennedy's involvement with Area 51 and UFOs. Reveals JFK's LSD experiences with Mary Pinchot-Meyer. The plot thickens with an ever expanding web of CIA involvement, from underground bases with UFOs seen by JFK and Marilyn Monroe (among others) to a vaster conspiracy that affects every government agency from NASA to the Justice Department. This may have been the reason that Marilyn Monroe and actress-columnist Dorothy Killgallen were both murdered. Focusing on the bizarre side of history, *Liquid Conspiracy* takes the reader on a psychedelic tour de force.
264 PAGES. 6x9 PAPERBACK. ILLUSTRATED. $14.95. CODE: LIQC

ATLANTIS: MOTHER OF EMPIRES
Atlantis Reprint Series
by Robert Stacy-Judd

Robert Stacy-Judd's classic 1939 book on Atlantis. Stacy-Judd was a California architect and an expert on the Mayas and their relationship to Atlantis. Stacy-Judd was an excellent artist and his book is lavishly illustrated. The eighteen comprehensive chapters in the book are: The Mayas and the Lost Atlantis; Conjectures and Opinions; The Atlantean Theory; Cro-Magnon Man; East Is West; And West Is East; The Mormons and the Mayas; Astrology in Two Hemispheres; The Language of Architecture; The American Indian; Pre-Panamanians and Pre-Incas; Columns and City Planning; Comparisons and Mayan Art; The Iberian Link; The Maya Tongue; Quetzalcoatl; Summing Up the Evidence; The Mayas in Yucatan.
340 PAGES. 8x11 PAPERBACK. ILLUSTRATED. INDEX. $19.95. CODE: AMOE

COSMIC MATRIX
Piece for a Jig-Saw, Part Two
by Leonard G. Cramp

Leonard G. Cramp, a British aerospace engineer, wrote his first book *Space Gravity and the Flying Saucer* in 1954. *Cosmic Matrix* is the long-awaited sequel to his 1966 book *UFOs & Anti-Gravity: Piece for a Jig-Saw*. Cramp has had a long history of examining UFO phenomena and has concluded that UFOs use the highest possible aeronautic science to move in the way they do. Cramp examines anti-gravity effects and theorizes that this super-science used by the craft—described in detail in the book—can lift mankind into a new level of technology, transportation and understanding of the universe. The book takes a close look at gravity control, time travel, and the interlocking web of energy between all planets in our solar system with Leonard's unique technical diagrams. A fantastic voyage into the present and future!
364 PAGES. 6x9 PAPERBACK. ILLUSTRATED. BIBLIOGRAPHY. $16.00. CODE: CMX

CONSPIRACY & HISTORY

HAARP
The Ultimate Weapon of the Conspiracy
by Jerry Smith
The HAARP project in Alaska is one of the most controversial projects ever undertaken by the U.S. Government. Jerry Smith gives us the history of the HAARP project and explains how it can be used as an awesome weapon of destruction. Smith exposes a covert military project and the web of conspiracies behind it. HAARP has many possible scientific and military applications, from raising a planetary defense shield to peering deep into the earth. Smith leads the reader down a trail of solid evidence into ever deeper and scarier conspiracy theories in an attempt to discover the "whos" and "whys" behind HAARP and discloses a possible plan to rule the world. At best, HAARP is science out-of-control; at worst, HAARP could be the most dangerous device ever created, a futuristic technology that is everything from super-beam weapon to world-wide mind control device. The Star Wars future is now. Topics include Over-the-Horizon Radar and HAARP, Mind Control, ELF and HAARP, The Telsa Connection, The Russian Woodpecker, GWEN & HAARP, Earth Penetrating Tomography, Weather Modification, Secret Science of the Conspiracy, more. Includes the complete 1987 Bernard Eastlund patent for his pulsed super-weapon that he claims was stolen by the HAARP Project.
256 PAGES. 6x9 PAPERBACK. ILLUSTRATED. $14.95. CODE: HARP

MIND CONTROL, OSWALD & JFK:
Were We Controlled?
Introduction by Kenn Thomas
Steamshovel Press editor Kenn Thomas examines the little-known book *Were We Controlled?*, first published in 1968. The book maintained that Lee Harvey Oswald was a special agent who was a mind control subject, having received an implant in 1960 at a Russian hospital. Thomas examines the evidence for implant technology and the role it could have played in the Kennedy Assassination. Thomas also looks at the mind control aspects of the RFK assassination and details the history of implant technology. A growing number of people are interested in CIA experiments and its "Silent Weapons for Quiet Wars."
256 PAGES. 6x9 PAPERBACK. ILLUSTRATED. NOTES. $16.00. CODE: MCOJ

MIND CONTROL, WORLD CONTROL
by Jim Keith
Veteran author and investigator Jim Keith uncovers a surprising amount of information on the technology, experimentation and implementation of mind control. Various chapters in this shocking book are on early CIA experiments such as Project Artichoke and Project R.H.I.C.-EDOM, the methodology and technology of implants, mind control assassins and couriers, various famous "Mind Control" victims such as Sirhan Sirhan and Candy Jones. Also featured in this book are chapters on how Mind Control technology may be linked to some UFO activity and "UFO abductions."
256 PAGES. 6x9 PAPERBACK. ILLUSTRATED. FOOTNOTES. $14.95. CODE: MCWC

PROJECT SEEK
Onassis, Kennedy and the Gemstone Thesis
by Gerald A. Carroll
This book reprints the famous Gemstone File, a document circulated in 1974 concerning the Mafia, Onassis and the Kennedy assassination. With the passing of Jackie Kennedy-Onassis, this information on the Mafia and the CIA, the formerly "Hughes" controlled defense industry, and the violent string of assassinations can at last be told. Also includes new information on the Nugan Hand Bank, the BCCI scandal, "the Octopus," and the Paul Wilcher Transcripts.
388 PAGES. 6x9 PAPERBACK. ILLUSTRATED. $16.95. CODE: PJS

NASA, NAZIS & JFK:
The Torbitt Document & the JFK Assassination
Introduction by Kenn Thomas
This book emphasizes the link between "Operation Paper Clip" Nazi scientists working for NASA, the assassination of JFK, and the secret Nevada air base Area 51. The Torbitt Document also talks about the roles played in the assassination by Division Five of the FBI, the Defense Industrial Security Command (DISC), the Las Vegas mob, and shadow corporate entities Permindex and Centro-Mondiale Commerciale. The Torbitt Document claims that the same players planned the 1962 assassination attempt on Charles de Gaul, who ultimately pulled out of NATO because he traced the "Assassination Cabal" to Permindex in Switzerland and to NATO headquarters in Brussels. The Torbitt Document paints a dark picture of NASA, the military industrial complex, and the connections to Mercury, Nevada which headquarters the "secret space program."
258 PAGES. 5x8. PAPERBACK. ILLUSTRATED. $16.00. CODE: NNJ

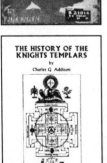

THE HISTORY OF THE KNIGHTS TEMPLARS
by
Charles G. Addison

Introduction by David Hatcher Childress

THE HISTORY OF THE KNIGHTS TEMPLAR
The Temple Church and the Temple
by Charles G. Addison. Introduction by David Hatcher Childress
Chapters on the origin of the Templars, their popularity in Europe and their rivalry with the Knights of St. John, later to be known as the Knights of Malta. Detailed information on the activities of the Templars in the Holy Land, and the 1312 A.D. suppression of the Templars in France and other countries, which culminated in the execution of Jacques de Molay and the continuation of the Knights Templars in England and Scotland and the formation of the society of Knights Templar in London and the rebuilding of the Temple in 1816. Plus a lengthy intro about the lost Templar fleet and its connections to the ancient North American sea routes.
395 PAGES. 6x9 PAPERBACK. ILLUSTRATED. $16.95. CODE: HKT

ATLANTIS REPRINT SERIES

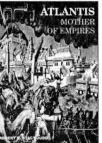

ATLANTIS: MOTHER OF EMPIRES
Atlantis Reprint Series
by Robert Stacy-Judd
Robert Stacy-Judd's classic 1939 book on Atlantis is back in print in this large-format paperback edition. Stacy-Judd was a California architect and an expert on the Mayas and their relationship to Atlantis. He was an excellent artist and his work is lavishly illustrated. The eighteen comprehensive chapters in the book are: The Mayas and the Lost Atlantis; Conjectures and Opinions; The Atlantean Theory; Cro-Magnon Man; East is West; And West is East; The Mormons and the Mayas; Astrology in Two Hemispheres; The Language of Architecture; The American Indian; Pre-Panamanians and Pre-Incas; Columns and City Planning; Comparisons and Mayan Art; The Iberian Link; The Maya Tongue; Quetzalcoatl; Summing Up the Evidence; The Mayas in Yucatan.
340 PAGES. 8X11 PAPERBACK. ILLUSTRATED. INDEX. $19.95. CODE: AMOE

SECRET CITIES OF OLD SOUTH AMERICA
Atlantis Reprint Series
by Harold T. Wilkins
The reprint of Wilkins' classic book, first published in 1952, claiming that South America was Atlantis. Chapters include Mysteries of a Lost World; Atlantis Unveiled; Red Riddles on the Rocks; South America's Amazons Existed!; The Mystery of El Dorado and Gran Payatiti—the Final Refuge of the Incas; Monstrous Beasts of the Unexplored Swamps & Wilds; Weird Denizens of Antediluvian Forests; New Light on Atlantis from the World's Oldest Book; The Mystery of Old Man Noah and the Arks; and more.
438 PAGES. 6X9 PAPERBACK. ILLUSTRATED. BIBLIOGRAPHY & INDEX. $16.95. CODE: SCOS

THE SHADOW OF ATLANTIS
The Echoes of Atlantean Civilization Tracked through Space & Time
by Colonel Alexander Braghine
First published in 1940, *The Shadow of Atlantis* is one of the great classics of Atlantis research. The book amasses a great deal of archaeological, anthropological, historical and scientific evidence in support of a lost continent in the Atlantic Ocean. Braghine covers such diverse topics as Egyptians in Central America, the myth of Quetzalcoatl, the Basque language and its connection with Atlantis, the connections with the ancient pyramids of Mexico, Egypt and Atlantis, the sudden demise of mammoths, legends of giants and much more. Braghine was a linguist and spends part of the book tracing ancient languages to Atlantis and studying little-known inscriptions in Brazil, deluge myths and the connections between ancient languages. Braghine takes us on a fascinating journey through space and time in search of the lost continent.
288 PAGES. 6X9 PAPERBACK. ILLUSTRATED. $16.95. CODE: SOA

THE SHADOW
OF ATLANTIS

ALEXANDER BRAGHINE

THIS 1940 CLASSIC ON ATLANTIS, MEXICO
AND ANCIENT 25 V PT IS BACK IN PRINT

ATLANTIS REPRINT SERIES

RIDDLE OF THE PACIFIC
by John Macmillan Brown
Oxford scholar Brown's classic work on lost civilizations of the Pacific is now back in print! John Macmillan Brown was an historian and New Zealand's premier scientist when he wrote about the origins of the Maoris. After many years of travel thoughout the Pacific studying the people and customs of the south seas islands, he wrote *Riddle of the Pacific* in 1924. The book is packed with rare turn-of-the-century illustrations. Don't miss Brown's classic study of Easter Island, ancient scripts, megalithic roads and cities, more. Brown was an early believer in a lost continent in the Pacific.
460 PAGES. 6X9 PAPERBACK. ILLUSTRATED. $16.95. CODE: ROP

THE RIDDLE OF
THE PACIFIC

JOHN MACMILLAN BROWN

This rare 1924 book is back in print!

THE HISTORY OF ATLANTIS
by Lewis Spence
Lewis Spence's classic book on Atlantis is now back in print! Spence was a Scottish historian (1874-1955) who is best known for his volumes on world mythology and his five Atlantis books. *The History of Atlantis* (1926) is considered his finest. Spence does his scholarly best in chapters on the Sources of Atlantean History, the Geography of Atlantis, the Races of Atlantis, the Kings of Atlantis, the Religion of Atlantis, the Colonies of Atlantis, more. Sixteen chapters in all.
240 PAGES. 6X9 PAPERBACK. ILLUSTRATED WITH MAPS, PHOTOS & DIAGRAMS. $16.95. CODE: HOA

ATLANTIS IN SPAIN
A Study of the Ancient Sun Kingdoms of Spain
by E.M. Whishaw
First published by Rider & Co. of London in 1928, this classic book is a study of the megaliths of Spain, ancient writing, cyclopean walls, sun worshipping empires, hydraulic engineering, and sunken cities. An extremely rare book, it was out of print for 60 years. Learn about the Biblical Tartessus; an Atlantean city at Niebla; the Temple of Hercules and the Sun Temple of Seville; Libyans and the Copper Age; more. Profusely illustrated with photos, maps and drawings.
284 PAGES. 6X9 PAPERBACK. ILLUSTRATED. TABLES OF ANCIENT SCRIPTS. $15.95. CODE: AIS

24 HOUR CREDIT CARD ORDERS—CALL: 815-253-6390 FAX: 815-253-6300
EMAIL: AUPHQ@FRONTIERNET.NET HTTP://WWW.ADVENTURESUNLIMITED.CO.NZ

MYSTIC TRAVELLER SERIES

THE MYSTERY OF EASTER ISLAND
by Katherine Routledge

The reprint of Katherine Routledge's classic archaeology book which was first published in London in 1919. Portions of book later appeared in *National Geographic* (1924). Heavily illustrated with a wealth of old photos, this book is a trea of information on that most mysterious of islands: Rapa Nui or Easter Island. The book details Katherine Routled journey by yacht from England to South America, around Patagonia to Chile and on to Easter Island. Routledge exple the amazing island and produced one of the first-ever accounts of the life, history and legends of this strange and rer place. Routledge discusses the statues, pyramid-platforms, Rongo Rongo script, the Bird Cult, the war between the S Ears and the Long Ears, the secret caves, ancient roads on the island, and more. This rare book serves as a sourcebook the early discoveries and theories on Easter Island. Original copies, when found, sell for hundreds of dollars so get this valuable reprint now at an affordable price.

432 PAGES. 6X9 PAPERBACK. ILLUSTRATED. $16.95. CODE: MEI

MYSTERY CITIES OF THE MAYA
Exploration and Adventure in Lubaantun & Belize
by Thomas Gann

First published in 1925, *Mystery Cities of the Maya* is a classic in Central American archae-ology-adventure. Gann was close friends with Mike Mitchell-Hedges, the British adven-turer who discovered the famous crystal skull with his adopted daughter Sammy and Lady Richmond Brown, their benefactress. Gann battles pirates along Belize's coast and goes upriver with Mitchell-Hedges to the site of Lubaantun where they excavate a strange lost city where the crystal skull was discovered. Lubaantun is a unique city in the Mayan world as it is built out of precisely carved blocks of stone without the usual plaster-cement facing. Lubaantun contained several large pyramids partially destroyed by earthquakes and a large amount of artifacts. Gann was a keen archaeologist, a member of the Mayan Society, and shared Michell-Hedges belief in Atlantis and lost civilizations (pre-Mayan), in Central America and the Caribbean. Lo good photos, maps and diagrams.

252 PAGES. 6X9 PAPERBACK. ILLUSTRATED. $16.95. CODE: MCOM

IN SECRET TIBET
by Theodore Illion

Reprint of a rare 30's travel book. Illion was a German traveller who not only spoke fluent Tibetan, but travelled in disguise through forbidden Tibet when it was off-limits to all out-siders. His incredible adventures make this one of the most exciting travel books ever pub-lished. Includes illustrations of Tibetan monks levitating stones by acoustics.

210 PAGES. 6X9 PAPERBACK. ILLUSTRATED. $15.95. CODE: IST

DARKNESS OVER TIBET
by Theodore Illion

In this second reprint of Illion's rare books, the German traveller continues his journey through Tibet and is given directions to a strange underground city. As the original publisher's remarks said, this is a rare account of an underground city in Tibet by the only Westerner ever to enter it and escape alive!

210 PAGES. 6X9 PAPERBACK. ILLUSTRATED. $15.95. CODE: DOT

IN SECRET MONGOLIA
by Henning Haslund

Danish-Swedish explorer Haslund's first book on his exciting explorations in Mongolia and Central Asia. Haslund tal via camel caravan to the medieval world of Mongolia, a country still barely known today. First published by Kegan P London in 1934, this rare travel adventure is back in print after 50 years. Haslund and his camel caravan journey acro Gobi Desert. He meets with renegade generals and warlords, god-kings and shamans. Haslund is captured, held for ran thrown into prison, battles black magic and portrays in vivid detail the birth of new nation. Haslund's second book *M Gods In Mongolia* is also available from Adventures Unlimited Press.

374 PAGES. 6X9 PAPERBACK. ILLUSTRATED. BIBLIOGRAPHY & INDEX. $16.95. CODE: ISM

MEN & GODS IN MONGOLIA
by Henning Haslund

First published in 1935 by Kegan Paul of London, Haslund takes us to the lost city of Karakota in the Gobi desert. We the Bodgo Gegen, a god-king in Mongolia similar to the Dalai Lama of Tibet. We meet Dambin Jansang, the dre warlord of the "Black Gobi." There is even material in this incredible book on the Hi-mori, an "airhorse" that flies thr the air (similar to a Vimana) and carries with it the sacred stone of Chintamani. Aside from the esoteric and mys material, there is plenty of just plain adventure: Haslund and companions journey across the Gobi desert by camel care are kidnapped and held for ransom; initiation into Shamanic societies; reincarnated warlords, and the violent bir "modern" Mongolia.

358 PAGES. 6X9 PAPERBACK. 57 PHOTOS, ILLUSTRATIONS AND MAPS. $15.95. CODE: MGM

UFOs & EXTRATERRESTRIALS

EXTRATERRESTRIAL ARCHAEOLOGY
by David Hatcher Childress

With 100s of photos and illustrations, *Extraterrestrial Archaeology* takes the reader to the strange and fascinating worlds of Mars, the Moon, Mercury, Venus, Saturn and other planets for a look at the alien structures that appear there. Using official NASA and Soviet photos, as well as other photos taken via telescope, this book seeks to prove that many of the planets (and moons) of our solar system are in some way inhabited by intelligent life. The book includes many blow-ups of NASA photos and detailed diagrams of structures—particularly on the Moon.
•NASA PHOTOS OF PYRAMIDS AND DOMED CITIES ON THE MOON.
•PYRAMIDS AND GIANT STATUES ON MARS.
•HOLLOW MOONS OF MARS AND OTHER PLANETS.
•ROBOT MINING VEHICLES THAT MOVE ABOUT THE MOON PROCESSING VALUABLE METALS.
•NASA & RUSSIAN PHOTOS OF SPACE-BASES ON MARS AND ITS MOONS.
•A BRITISH SCIENTIST WHO DISCOVERED A TUNNEL ON THE MOON, AND OTHER "BOTTOMLESS CRATERS."
•EARLY CLAIMS OF TRIPS TO THE MOON AND MARS.
•STRUCTURAL ANOMALIES ON VENUS, SATURN, JUPITER, MERCURY,URANUS & NEPTUNE.
•NASA, THE MOON AND ANTI-GRAVITY. PLUS MORE. HIGHLY ILLUSTRATED WITH PHOTOS, DIAGRAMS AND MAPS!
304 PAGES. 8x11 PAPERBACK. BIBLIOGRAPHY & APPENDIX. $18.95. CODE: ETA

THE CASE FOR THE FACE
Scientists Examine the Evidence for Alien Artifacts on Mars
edited by Stanley McDaniel and Monica Rix Paxson
Mars Imagery by Mark Carlotto

The ultimate compendium on artificial structures in the Cydonia region of Mars. *The Case For the Face* unifies the research and opinions of a remarkably accomplished group of scientists, including a former NASA astronaut, a quantum physicist who is the chair of a space science program, leading meteor researchers, nine Ph.D.'s, the best-selling science author in Germany and more. The book includes: NASA research proving we're not the first intelligent race in this solar system; 120 amazing high resolution images never seen before by the general public; three separate doctoral statistical studies demonstrating the likelihood of artificial objects at the Cydonian site to be over 99%; and other definitive proof of life on Mars. Solid science presented in a readable, richly illustrated format. Featured on the Learning Channel with Leonard Nimoy.
320 PAGES. 6x9 PAPERBACK. ILLUSTRATED. INDEX & BIBLIOGRAPHY. $17.95. CODE: CFF

FLYING SAUCERS OVER LOS ANGELES
The UFO Craze of the '50s
by DeWayne B. Johnson & Kenn Thomas
commentary by David Hatcher Childress

Beginning with a previously unpublished manuscript written in the early 1950s by DeWayne B. Johnson entitled "Flying Saucers Over Los Angeles," this book chronicles the earliest flying saucer flap beginning June 24, 1947. The book continues with other sightings into the late '50s, including many rare photos. It also presents one of the first analyses of the sociological and psychological dimensions of the UFO experience, from a vantage point of certainty that flying saucers are real—borne out by the actual news and witness accounts. Starting with such cases as the Roswell crash and the Maury Island incident, it continues to little-known sightings; this manuscript offers a contemporaneous view of the earliest UFO excitement in America, unvarnished by the accumulated speculation of the last 50 years. A more detailed account of the many early sightings has never before been published. Additionally, the book contains an appendix of actual newsclippings from the Los Angeles newspapers of the time.
256 PAGES. 6x9 PAPERBACK. ILLUSTRATED. BIBLIOGRAPHY. $16.00. CODE: FSLA

COEVOLUTION
The True Story of 10 Days with an Extraterrestrial Civilization
by Alec Newald

One Monday in mid-February 1989, Alec Newald set off on what should have been a 3-hour drive from Rotorua to Auckland but instead became 10 days of missing time! Newald claims he had been taken by friendly aliens to their home planet during this time. In the first part of the book he describes the planet, the civilization and the technology used by these extraterrestrials. The second part of the book is about the strange visitations that he received from "government scientists" who wanted to know what he knew about ET's, and the profound implications for planet earth: coevolution with another world.
194 PAGES. 5x8 PAPERBACK. ILLUSTRATED. APPENDIX. $16.95. CODE: COEV

PYRAMID TRUTH GATEWAY UNIVERSE
The Purpose, Intent, and Overview of Extraterrestrial Visitations
by Reg T. Miller

A thick and well-illustrated book on the mysteries of the Great Pyramid and how this ancient structure relates with space travel, time travel and extraterrestrials. Lots of diagrams and sacred geometry are used to explain: The Origin of Creation; Ancient Civilizations and Technology; Earth Chronicles; Abductions and Implants; Transitions and Time Warps; Pyramid Power; Ancient Astronauts; Energy Healing; Nemesis, the Deadly Comet; more.
359 PAGES. 7x10 PAPERBACK. ILLUSTRATED. $24.95. CODE: PTGU

24 HOUR CREDIT CARD ORDERS—CALL: 815-253-6390 FAX: 815-253-6300
EMAIL: AUPHQ@FRONTIERNET.NET HTTP://WWW.ADVENTURESUNLIMITED.CO.NZ

ANTI-GRAVITY

THE ANTI-GRAVITY HANDBOOK

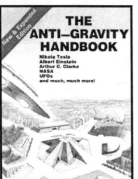

THE ANTI-GRAVITY HANDBOOK
Nikola Tesla
Albert Einstein
Arthur C. Clarke
NASA
UFOs
and much, much more!

edited by David Hatcher Childress, with Nikola Tesla, T.B. Paulicki, Bruce Cathie, Albert Einstein and others

The new expanded compilation of material on Anti-Gravity, Free Energy, Flying Saucer Propulsion, UFOs, Suppressed Technology, NASA Cover-ups and more. Highly illustrated with patents, technical illustrations and photos. This revised and expanded edition has more material, including photos of Area 51, Nevada, the government's secret testing facility. This classic on weird science is back in a 90s format!

• How to build a flying saucer.
• Arthur C. Clarke on Anti-Gravity.
• Crystals and their role in levitation.
• Secret government research and development.
• Nikola Tesla on how anti-gravity airships could
  draw power from the atmosphere.
• Bruce Cathie's Anti-Gravity Equation.
• NASA, the Moon and Anti-Gravity.
230 PAGES. 7x10 PAPERBACK. BIBLIOGRAPHY/INDEX/APPENDIX. HIGHLY ILLUSTRATED.
$14.95. CODE: AGH

ANTI-GRAVITY & THE WORLD GRID

edited by David Hatcher Childress

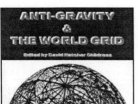

Is the earth surrounded by an intricate electromagnetic grid network offering free energy? This compilation of material on ley lines and world power points contains chapters on the geography, mathematics, and light harmonics of the earth grid. Learn the purpose of ley lines and ancient megalithic structures located on the grid. Discover how the grid made the Philadelphia Experiment possible. Explore the Coral Castle and many other mysteries, including acoustic levitation, Tesla Shields and scalar wave weaponry. Browse through the section on anti-gravity patents, and research resources.
274 PAGES. 7x10 PAPERBACK. ILLUSTRATED. $14.95. CODE: AGW

ANTI-GRAVITY & THE UNIFIED FIELD

edited by David Hatcher Childress

Is Einstein's Unified Field Theory the answer to all of our energy problems? Explored in this compilation of material is how gravity, electricity and magnetism manifest from a unified field around us. Why artificial gravity is possible; secrets of UFO propulsion; free energy; Nikola Tesla and anti-gravity airships of the 20s and 30s; flying saucers as superconducting whirls of plasma; anti-mass generators; vortex propulsion; suppressed technology; government cover-ups; gravitational pulse drive; spacecraft & more.
240 PAGES. 7x10 PAPERBACK. ILLUSTRATED. $14.95. CODE: AGU

Forward astronaut Capt. Edgar D. Mitchell, Ph. D.

ETHER-TECHNOLOGY
A Rational Approach to Gravity Control

by Rho Sigma
THE UNDERGROUND CLASSIC IS BACK IN PRINT

ETHER TECHNOLOGY

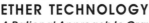

A Rational Approach to Gravity Control
by Rho Sigma

This classic book on anti-gravity and free energy is back in print and back in stock. Written by a well-known American scientist under the pseudonym of "Rho Sigma," this book delves into international efforts at gravity control and discoid craft propulsion. Before the Quantum Field there was "Ether." This small, but informative book has chapters on John Searle and "Sea discs;" T. Townsend Brown and his work on anti-gravity and ether-vortex turbines. Includes forward by former NASA astronaut Edgar Mitchell.
108 PAGES. 6x9 PAPERBACK. ILLUSTRATED. $12.95. CODE: ETT

ANTI-GRAVITY AND THE UNIFIED FIELD
Edited by David Hatcher Childress

Albert Einstein
Nikola Tesla
T. Townsend Brown
Gravity Control
UFOs
Vortex Technology
Electro-Gravitic Propulsion
& Much, much more.

TAPPING THE ZERO POINT ENERGY

Free Energy & Anti-Gravity in Today's Physics
by Moray B. King

King explains how free energy and anti-gravity are possible. The theories of the zero point energy maintain there is tremendous fluctuations of electrical field energy imbedded within the fabric of space. This book tells how, in the 1930s, inventor T. Henry Moray could produce a fifty kilowatt "free energy" machine; how an electrified plasma vortex creates anti-gravity; how the Pons/Fleischmann "cold fusion" experiment could produce tremendous heat without fusion; and how certain experiments might produce a gravitational anomaly.
170 PAGES. 5x8 PAPERBACK. ILLUSTRATED. $9.95. CODE: TAP

ANTI-GRAVITY

THE FREE-ENERGY DEVICE HANDBOOK
A Compilation of Patents & Reports

THE FREE-ENERGY DEVICE HANDBOOK
A Compilation of Patents and Reports
by David Hatcher Childress
A large-format compilation of various patents, papers, descriptions and diagrams concerning free-energy devices and systems. *The Free-Energy Device Handbook* is a visual tool for experimenters and researchers into magnetic motors and other "over-unity" devices. With chapters on the Adams Motor, the Hans Coler Generator, cold fusion, superconductors, "N" machines, space-energy generators, Nikola Tesla, T. Townsend Brown, and the latest in free-energy devices. Packed with photos, technical diagrams, patents and fascinating information, this book belongs on every science shelf. With energy and profit being a major political reason for fighting various wars, free-energy devices, if ever allowed to be mass distributed to consumers, could change the world! Get your copy now before the Department of Energy bans this book!
292 PAGES. 8X10 PAPERBACK. ILLUSTRATED. BIBLIOGRAPHY. $16.95. CODE: FEH

UNDER GROUND
Bases and Tunnels
What is the government trying to hide?
Richard Sauder, Ph.D.

UNDERGROUND BASES & TUNNELS
What is the Government Trying to Hide?
by Richard Sauder, Ph.D.
Working from government documents and corporate records, Sauder has compiled an impressive book that digs below the surface of the military's super-secret underground! Go behind the scenes into little-known corners of the public record and discover how corporate America has worked hand-in-glove with the Pentagon for decades, dreaming about, planning, and actually constructing, secret underground bases. This book includes chapters on the locations of the bases, the tunneling technology, various military designs for underground bases, nuclear testing & underground bases, abductions, needles & implants, military involvement in "alien" cattle mutilations, more. 50 page photo & map insert.
201 PAGES. 6X9 PAPERBACK. ILLUSTRATED. $15.95. CODE: UGB

UFOS and ANTI-GRAVITY:
PIECE FOR A JIG-SAW
by Leonard G. Cramp

UFOS AND ANTI-GRAVITY
Piece For A Jig-Saw
by Leonard G. Cramp
Leonard G. Cramp's 1966 classic book on flying saucer propulsion and suppressed technology is available again. *UFOS & Anti-Gravity: Piece For A Jig-Saw* is a highly technical look at the UFO phenomena by a trained scientist. Cramp first introduces the idea of 'anti-gravity' and introduces us to the various theories of gravitation. He then examines the technology necessary to build a flying saucer and examines in great detail the technical aspects of such a craft. Cramp's book is a wealth of material and diagrams on flying saucers, anti-gravity, suppressed technology, G-fields and UFOs. Chapters include Crossroads of Aerodymanics, Aerodynamic Saucers, Limitations of Rocketry, Gravitation and the Ether, Gravitational Spaceships, G-Field Lift Effects, The Bi-Field Theory, VTOL and Hovercraft, Analysis of UFO photos, more. "I feel the Air Force has not been giving out all available information on these unidentified flying objects. You cannot disregard so many unimpeachable sources." — John McCormack, Speaker of the U.S. House of Representatives.
388 PAGES. 6X9 PAPERBACK. HEAVILY ILLUSTRATED. $16.95. CODE: UAG

MAN-MADE UFOS 1944—1994
Fifty Years of Suppression
by Renato Vesco & David Hatcher Childress
A comprehensive look at the early "flying saucer" technology of Nazi Germany and the genesis of man-made UFOs. This book takes us from the work of captured German scientists to escaped battalions of Germans, secret communities in South America and Antarctica to todays state-of-the-art "Dreamland" flying machines. Heavily illustrated, this astonishing book blows the lid off the "government UFO conspiracy" and explains with technical diagrams the technology involved. Examined in detail are secret underground airfields and factories; German secret weapons; "suction" aircraft; the origin of NASA; gyroscopic stabilizers and engines; the secret Marconi aircraft factory in South America; and more. Not to be missed by students of technology suppression, secret societies, anti-gravity, free energy conspiracy and World War II! Introduction by W.A. Harbinson, author of the Dell novels *GENESIS* and *REVELATION*.
318 PAGES. 6X9 PAPERBACK. ILLUSTRATED. INDEX & FOOTNOTES. $18.95. CODE: MMU

Man-Made UFOS
1944-1994
50 Years of Suppression
Renato Vesco & David Hatcher Childress

THE COMING ENERGY REVOLUTION
THE SEARCH FOR FREE ENERGY
JEANE MANNING

THE COMING ENERGY REVOLUTION
The Search For Free Energy
by Jeane Manning
Free energy researcher and journalist Jeane Manning takes us for a great look at the breakthrough technologies, inventions and inventors that will change the way we live. Chapters on Nikola Tesla; Solid-State Energy Devices and their Inventors; Floyd Sweet—Solid State Magnet Pioneer; Rotating-Magnet Energy Innovators; Cold Fusion; Hydrogen Power; Low-Impact Water Power—A New Twist on an Old Technology; Harassing the Energy Innovators. 15 chapters in all.
230 PAGES. 6X9 PAPERBACK. ILLUSTRATED. GLOSSARY, BIBLIOGRAPHY, INDEX. $12.95. CODE: CER

---

24 HOUR CREDIT CARD ORDERS—CALL: 815-253-6390 FAX: 815-253-6300
EMAIL: AUPHQ@FRONTIERNET.NET HTTP://WWW.ADVENTURESUNLIMITED.CO.NZ

THE LOST CITIES SERIES

LOST CITIES OF ATLANTIS, ANCIENT EUROPE & THE MEDITERRANEAN
by David Hatcher Childress

Atlantis! The legendary lost continent comes under the close scrutiny of maverick archaeologist David Hatcher Childress in sixth book in the internationally popular *Lost Cities* series. Childress takes the reader in search of sunken cities in the Medit nean; across the Atlas Mountains in search of Atlantean ruins; to remote islands in search of megalithic ruins; to meet l legends and secret societies. From Ireland to Turkey, Morocco to Eastern Europe, and around the remote islands of the Medit nean and Atlantic, Childress takes the reader on an astonishing quest for mankind's past. Ancient technology, cataclysms, m lithic construction, lost civilizations and devastating wars of the past are all explored in this book. Childress challenges the ske and proves that great civilizations not only existed in the past, but the modern world and its problems are reflections of the an world of Atlantis.

524 PAGES. 6X9 PAPERBACK. ILLUSTRATED WITH 100S OF MAPS, PHOTOS AND DIAGRAMS. BI OGRAPHY & INDEX. $16.95. CODE: MED

LOST CITIES OF CHINA, CENTRAL INDIA & ASIA
by David Hatcher Childress

Like a real life "Indiana Jones," maverick archaeologist David Childress takes the reader on an incredible adventure a some of the world's oldest and most remote countries in search of lost cities and ancient mysteries. Discover ancient citie in the Gobi Desert; hear fantastic tales of lost continents, vanished civilizations and secret societies bent on ruling the world; visit forgotten monasteries in forbidding snow-capped mountains with strange tunnels to mysterious subterranean cities! A unique combination of far-out exploration and practical travel advice, it will astound and delight the experienced traveler or the armchair voyager.

429 PAGES. 6X9 PAPERBACK. ILLUSTRATED. FOOTNOTES & BIBLIOGRAPHY. $14.95. CODE: CHI

LOST CITIES OF ANCIENT LEMURIA & THE PACIFIC
by David Hatcher Childress

Was there once a continent in the Pacific? Called Lemuria or Pacifica by geologists, Mu or Pan by the mystics, there is now ample mythological, geological and archaeological evidence to "prove" that an advanced and ancient civilization once lived in the central Pacific. Maverick archaeologist and explorer David Hatcher Childress combs the Indian Ocean, Australia and the Pacific in search of the surprising truth about mankind's past. Contains photos of the underwater city on Pohnpei; explanations on how the statues were levitated around Easter Island in a clockwise vortex movement; tales of disappearing islands; Egyptians in Australia; and more.

379 PAGES. 6X9 PAPERBACK. ILLUSTRATED. FOOTNOTES & BIBLIOGRAPHY. $14.95. CODE: L

ANCIENT TONGA
& the Lost City of Mu'a
by David Hatcher Childress

Lost Cities series author Childress takes us to the south sea islands of Tonga, Rarotonga, Samoa and Fiji to investigate the megalithic ruins on these beautiful islands. The great empire of the Polynesians, centered on Tonga and the ancient city of Mu'a, is revealed with old photos, drawings and maps. Chapters in this book are on the Lost City of Mu'a and its many megalithic pyramids, the Ha'amonga Trilithon and ancient Polynesian astronomy, Samoa and the search for the lost land of Havai'iki, Fiji and its wars with Tonga, Rarotonga's megalithic road, and Polynesian cosmology. Material on Egyptians in the Pacific, earth changes, the fortified moat around Mu'a, lost roads, more.

218 PAGES. 6X9 PAPERBACK. ILLUSTRATED. COLOR PHOTOS. BIBLIOGRAPHY. $15.95. CODE: TONG

ANCIENT MICRONESIA
& the Lost City of Nan Madol
by David Hatcher Childress

Micronesia, a vast archipelago of islands west of Hawaii and south of Japan, contains some of the most amazing mega ruins in the world. Part of our *Lost Cities* series, this volume explores the incredible conformations on various Micron islands, especially the fantastic and little-known ruins of Nan Madol on Pohnpei Island. The huge canal city of Nan N contains over 250 million tons of basalt columns over an 11 square-mile area of artificial islands. Much of the huge c submerged, and underwater structures can be found to an estimated 80 feet. Islanders' legends claim that the basalt r weighing up to 50 tons, were magically levitated into place by the powerful forefathers. Other ruins in Micronesia th profiled include the Latte Stones of the Marianas, the menhirs of Palau, the megalithic canal city on Kosrae Island, meg on Guam, and more.

256 PAGES. 6X9 PAPERBACK. ILLUSTRATED. INCLUDES A COLOR PHOTO SECTION. BIBLIOGRA $16.95. CODE: AMIC

THE LOST CITIES SERIES

VIMANA AIRCRAFT OF ANCIENT INDIA & ATLANTIS
by David Hatcher Childress
introduction by Ivan T. Sanderson
Did the ancients have the technology of flight? In this incredible volume on ancient India, authentic Indian texts such as the *Ramayana* and the *Mahabharata* are used to prove that ancient aircraft were in use more than four thousand years ago. Included in this book is the entire Fourth Century BC manuscript *Vimaanika Shastra* by the ancient author Maharishi Bharadwaaja, translated into English by the Mysore Sanskrit professor G.R. Josyer. Also included are chapters on Atlantean technology, the incredible Rama Empire of India and the devastating wars that destroyed it. Also an entire chapter on mercury vortex propulsion and mercury gyros, the power source described in the ancient Indian texts. Not to be missed by those interested in ancient civilizations or the UFO enigma.
334 PAGES. 6X9 PAPERBACK. RARE PHOTOGRAPHS, MAPS AND DRAWINGS. $15.95. CODE: VAA

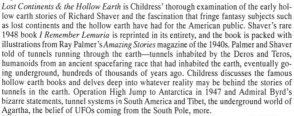
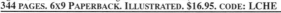

LOST CONTINENTS & THE HOLLOW EARTH
I Remember Lemuria and the Shaver Mystery
by David Hatcher Childress & Richard Shaver

Lost Continents & the Hollow Earth is Childress' thorough examination of the early hollow earth stories of Richard Shaver and the fascination that fringe fantasy subjects such as lost continents and the hollow earth have had for the American public. Shaver's rare 1948 book *I Remember Lemuria* is reprinted in its entirety, and the book is packed with illustrations from Ray Palmer's *Amazing Stories* magazine of the 1940s. Palmer and Shaver told of tunnels running through the earth—tunnels inhabited by the Deros and Teros, humanoids from an ancient spacefaring race that had inhabited the earth, eventually going underground, hundreds of thousands of years ago. Childress discusses the famous hollow earth books and delves deep into whatever reality may be behind the stories of tunnels in the earth. Operation High Jump to Antarctica in 1947 and Admiral Byrd's bizarre statements, tunnel systems in South America and Tibet, the underground world of Agartha, the belief of UFOs coming from the South Pole, more.
344 PAGES. 6X9 PAPERBACK. ILLUSTRATED. $16.95. CODE: LCHE

LOST CITIES OF NORTH & CENTRAL AMERICA
by David Hatcher Childress
Down the back roads from coast to coast, maverick archaeologist and adventurer David Hatcher Childress goes deep into unknown America. With this incredible book, you will search for lost Mayan cities and books of gold, discover an ancient canal system in Arizona, climb gigantic pyramids in the Midwest, explore megalithic monuments in New England, and join the astonishing quest for lost cities throughout North America. From the war-torn jungles of Guatemala, Nicaragua and Honduras to the deserts, mountains and fields of Mexico, Canada, and the U.S.A., Childress takes the reader in search of sunken ruins, Viking forts, strange tunnel systems, living dinosaurs, early Chinese explorers, and fantastic lost treasure. Packed with both early and current maps, photos and illustrations.
590 PAGES. 6X9 PAPERBACK. PHOTOS, MAPS, AND ILLUSTRATIONS. FOOTNOTES & BIBLIOGRAPHY. $14.95. CODE: NCA

LOST CITIES & ANCIENT MYSTERIES OF SOUTH AMERICA
by David Hatcher Childress
Rogue adventurer and maverick archaeologist David Hatcher Childress takes the reader on unforgettable journeys deep into deadly jungles, high up on windswept mountains and across scorching deserts in search of lost civilizations and ancient mysteries. Travel with David and explore stone cities high in mountain forests and hear fantastic tales of Inca treasure, living dinosaurs, and a mysterious tunnel system. Whether he is hopping freight trains, searching for secret cities, or just dealing with the daily problems of food, money, and romance, the author keeps the reader spellbound. Includes both early and current maps, photos, and illustrations, and plenty of advice for the explorer planning his or her own journey of discovery.
381 PAGES. 6X9 PAPERBACK. PHOTOS, MAPS, AND ILLUSTRATIONS. FOOTNOTES & BIBLIOGRAPHY. $14.95. CODE: SAM

LOST CITIES & ANCIENT MYSTERIES OF AFRICA & ARABIA
by David Hatcher Childress
Across ancient deserts, dusty plains and steaming jungles, maverick archaeologist David Childress continues his world-wide quest for lost cities and ancient mysteries. Join him as he discovers forbidden cities in the Empty Quarter of Arabia; "Atlantean" ruins in Egypt and the Kalahari desert; a mysterious, ancient empire in the Sahara; and more. This is the tale of an extraordinary life on the road: across war-torn countries, Childress searches for King Solomon's Mines, living dinosaurs, the Ark of the Covenant and the solutions to some of the fantastic mysteries of the past.
423 PAGES. 6X9 PAPERBACK. PHOTOS, MAPS, AND ILLUSTRATIONS. FOOTNOTES & BIBLIOGRAPHY. $14.95. CODE: AFA

24 HOUR CREDIT CARD ORDERS—CALL: 815-253-6390 FAX: 815-253-6300
EMAIL: AUPHQ@FRONTIERNET.NET HTTP://WWW.ADVENTURESUNLIMITED.CO.NZ

MIND CONTROL AND UFOS
Casebook on Alternative 3
by Jim Keith

A revised and updated edition of *Casebook on Alternative 3*, Keith's classic investigation of the Alternative 3 scenario first appeared on British television over 20 years ago. Keith delves into the bizarre story of Alternative 3, including control programs, underground bases not only on the Earth but also on the Moon and Mars, the real origin of the problem, the mysterious deaths of Marconi Electronics employees in Britain during the 1980s, the Russian-American s power arms race of the 50s, 60s and 70s as a massive hoax, more.

248 PAGES. 6X9 PAPERBACK. ILLUSTRATED. $14.95. CODE: MCUF

WHO MURDERED YITZHAK RABIN?
The Shocking Treachery that Altered the Face of History
by Barry Chamish

Israeli investigator Barry Chamish asks whether it was a right-wing loner that shot Prime Minister Yitzhak Rabin on No ber 4, 1995? Bar Ilan University student Yigal Amir was immediately arrested and later convicted of this murder. Cha reveals disturbing evidence that a larger conspiracy was involved and names the actual killers and their sloppy conspira the scene, witnesses heard bodyguards and policemen shouting, "They're blanks! They're blanks!"; the "amateur" film assassination, as well as eyewitness testimony, documents that Rabin appeared relatively unhurt by the shots; the footage clearly shows that a back door of Rabin's empty limousine was slammed shut from inside before he was pushed the vehicle. Who was waiting for him and why did they take an unnecessarily long trip to the hospital?

146 PAGES. 6X9 PAPERBACK. ILLUSTRATED. $12.95. CODE: WMYR

PAN AM 103
The Lockerbie Cover-Up
by William C. Chasey

According to William Chasey, there is a cover-up occurring over the Lockerbie disaster that makes "Watergate, Irangat Whitewater pale by comparison." Casey claims that the United States and Great Britain have conspired to keep the perpetrators from being exposed while they falsely accuse Libya. Chasey discloses the cover-up and names the real p responsible.

372 PAGES. 6X9 PAPERBACK. ILLUSTRATED. INDEX. $17.95. CODE: PA3

SPIES, TRAITORS AND MOLES
by Peter Kross

Most Americans do not know the true story of spying and covert activities in American History. The use of spies to fu American foreign and domestic policy has its roots in the American Revolution. Spies are everywhere, for good or fo (depending which side you are on...). Covert actions have influenced this nation's quest for international superiorit continue to the present time. Kross tells the tales of the extraordinary men and women whose covert activities helped pa way for America's dominance in world affairs.

260 PAGES. 6X9 PAPERBACK. ILLUSTRATED. $14.95. CODE: STM

DIPLOMACY BY DECEPTION
by Dr. John Coleman

British conspiracy writer Dr. John Coleman with this exposé on the secret machinations of the British and American alli and how their citizens are deceived by the detrimental policies of these governments. Coleman gives fascinating acc and sheds new light on such diverse operations as the Gulf War; the Bolshevik Revolution; the murder of Martin Luther King; the creation of an artificial Saudi Arabian client state for the oil industry; the rape of Mexico by British and American oil barons; the invasion of Panama; how the U.N. is used as a war-making body; more.

267 PAGES. 6X9 PAPERBACK. ILLUSTRATED. $16.95. CODE: DBD

SAUCERS OF THE ILLUMINATI
by Jim Keith

Seeking the truth behind stories of alien invasion, secret underground bases, and the secret plans of the New World Order, *Saucers of the Illuminati* offers groundbreaking research, uncovering clues to the nature of UFOs and to forces even more sinister: the secret cabal behind planetary control! Includes mind control, saucer abductions, cattle mutilations, government anti-gravity testing, plus more from veteran conspiracy and UFO author Keith.

130 PAGES. 6X9 PAPERBACK. $12.95. CODE: SOIL

THE IMMACULATE DECEPTION
The Bush Crime Family Exposed
by Russell S. Bowen

The book explores the serious question of George Bush's whereabouts (1)when the Bay of Pigs fiasco was planned and exec (2)when John F. Kennedy, Martin Luther King and Robert F. Kennedy were assassinated?; (3)when Ronald Reagan was assassinated in Washington by a known Bush family associate. Plus the early CIA years; Prescot Bush sold aviation fuel Nazis; more.

210 PAGES. 5X8 PAPERBACK. $12.95. CODE: TID

DIPLOMA BY DECEPTIC

AN ACCOUNT OF TH TREASONOUS CONDUC BY THE GOVERNMENTS OF BRITAIN AND THE UNITED STATES

DR. JOHN COLEMA

STEAMSHOVEL PRESS

Acharya S
Greg Bishop
Len Bracken
David Hatcher Childress
Uri Dowbenko
Wayne Henderson
Jim Keith
Jim Martin
Adam Parfrey
Rob Sterling

The names of the world's best conspiracy culture researchers appear regularly in the pages of *Steamshovel Press*.

Steamshovel examines parapolitical topics in the tradition Mae Brussell, Jim Garrison, Ace Hayes and Danny Casolaro, exploring the many strange dimensions of the contemporary Con. From the UFO cover up to the politics of assassination, the religious hucksters and the corporate/military nightmare, *Steamshovel Press* covers it all with dependable and complete documentation.

"Feed that dark feeling in the pit of your belly."
--Arcturus Books

"...on the cutting edge--and a strange place that is...:
--*New Yorker*

Don't miss an issue--or the Conspiracy will close in on you! $6 per sample issue; $23 for a four issue subscription.

Checks payable to "Kenn Thomas" at POB 23715, St. Louis, MO 63121

On the web at www.umsl.edu/~skthoma

One Adventure Place
P.O. Box 74
Kempton, Illinois 60946
United States of America
Tel.: 815-253-6390 • Fax: 815-253-6300
Email: auphq@frontiernet.net
http://www.adventuresunlimitedpress.com
or www.adventuresunlimited.nl

ORDERING INSTRUCTIONS

✓ Remit by USD$ Check, Money Order or Credit Card

✓ Visa, Master Card, Discover & AmEx Accepted

✓ Prices May Change Without Notice

✓ 10% Discount for 3 or more Items

SHIPPING CHARGES

United States

✓ Postal Book Rate { $3.00 First Item
50¢ Each Additional Item

✓ Priority Mail { $4.00 First Item
$2.00 Each Additional Item

✓ UPS { $5.00 First Item
$1.50 Each Additional Item

NOTE: UPS Delivery Available to Mainland USA Only

Canada

✓ Postal Book Rate { $6.00 First Item
$2.00 Each Additional Item

✓ Postal Air Mail { $8.00 First Item
$2.50 Each Additional Item

✓ Personal Checks or Bank Drafts MUST BE

USD$ and Drawn on a US Bank
✓ Canadian Postal Money Orders OK

✓Payment MUST BE USD$

All Other Countries

✓ Surface Delivery { $10.00 First Item
$4.00 Each Additional Item

✓ Postal Air Mail { $14.00 First Item
$5.00 Each Additional Item

✓Payment MUST BE USD$

✓ Checks and Money Orders MUST BE USD$
and Drawn on a US Bank or branch.

✓ Add $5.00 for Air Mail Subscription to
Future *Adventures Unlimited* Catalogs

SPECIAL NOTES

✓ RETAILERS: Standard Discounts Available

✓ BACKORDERS: We Backorder all Out-of-
Stock Items Unless Otherwise Requested

✓ PRO FORMA INVOICES: Available on Request

✓VIDEOS: NTSC Mode Only. Replacement only.

✓ For PAL mode videos contact our other offices:

Please check: ☑

☐ This is my first order   ☐ I have ordered before

Name				
Address				
City				
State/Province			Postal Code	
Country				
Phone day		Evening		
Fax				

Item Code	Item Description	Qty	Total

Please check: ☑

		Subtotal ➟	
	Less Discount-10% for 3 or more items ➟		
☐ Postal-Surface	Balance ➟		
☐ Postal-Air Mail (Priority in USA)	Illinois Residents 6.25% Sales Tax ➟		
	Previous Credit ➟		
☐ UPS	Shipping ➟		
(Mainland USA only)	Total (check/MO in USD$ only)➟		

☐ Visa/MasterCard/Discover/Amex

Card Number

Expiration Date

10% Discount When You Order 3 or More Items!